JAN P. KRENTZ

Quick Star Quilts
& BEYOND

20 Dazzling Projects • Classroom-Tested Techniques • Galaxy of Inspiration

C&T PUBLISHING

Text copyright © 2009 by Jan P. Krentz

Artwork copyright © 2009 by C&T Publishing, Inc.

Publisher: Amy Marson

Creative Director: Gailen Runge

Editors: Karla Menaugh and Kesel Wilson

Technical Editors: Ellen Pahl and Mary E. Flynn

Copyeditor/Proofreader: Wordfirm Inc.

Cover Designer: Kristen Yenche

Book Designer: Rose Sheifer-Wright

Production Coordinator: Zinnia Heinzmann

Illustrator: Gregg Valley

Photography by Luke Mulks, Diane Pedersen, and Christina Carty-Francis of
C&T Publishing unless otherwise noted

Published by C&T Publishing, Inc., P.O. Box 1456, Lafayette, CA 94549

Library of Congress Cataloging-in-Publication Data

Krentz, Jan P.,

  Quick star quilts & beyond : 20 dazzling projects, classroom-tested techniques, galaxy of inspiration / Jan P. Krentz.

     p. cm.

  "Detailed geometric patterns with diamonds and set-in seams can be daunting. This book introduces the shapes and techniques in a simple format. The basis for the designs in this collection is the 45° diamond, or parallelogram"--Provided by publisher.

  ISBN 978-1-57120-510-0 (paper trade : alk. paper)

  1. Patchwork--Patterns. 2. Quilting--Patterns. 3. Star quilts. I. Title. II. Title: Quick star quilts and beyond.

  TT835.K7685 2009

  746.46'041--dc22

                        2008025492

Printed in China

10 9 8 7 6 5 4 3 2

Acknowledgments

My sincerest appreciation to the fine editors and designers at C&T Publishing! My sincerest appreciation also goes to Karla Menaugh for her organization and guidance, Ellen Pahl for her critical eye and accurate calculations, and Kesel Wilson for overseeing the entire manuscript. My personal thanks to Jan Grigsby, who has been with C&T during the writing of all four of my books—enjoy your next life adventures! Thank you, Amy Marson, Gailen Runge, Kristen Yenche, and Rose Sheifer-Wright for your creative contributions to this book! Recognition and thanks to Luke Mulks, Diane Pedersen, and Christina Carty-Francis for their beautiful photography.

Many quiltmakers have shared their quilts in this book—and my thanks go to Betty Alofs, Anna Mae Bach, Mona Baran, Jenny Bowker, Kathy Butler, Darlene Christopherson, and members of the Homespun Quilters Guild (Waco, Texas), Kim Farmer, Marcia Harlamert, Pam Kay, Jacqueline Lacey, Rebecca Lighthill, Lynne Lichtenstern, Lorraine Marstall, Christine Porter, Ann Sidell, Patricia Votruba, J. Michelle Watts, Amy Wazny, Pat Wolfe, and Julia Zgliniec. A special thank you to machine quilters Debra Geissler, Carolyn Reynolds, Janet Sturdevant Stuart, Sue Mezera, and Susanne Fagot—you make my quilts "sing"!

Dedication

This book is dedicated to my husband, Don, and my children, Ryan, Dan, and Lindsay. Thank you for your love and support!

Contents

INTRODUCTION

I enjoy making and using quilts! Traditional pieced designs are especially appealing to me, and pieced patterns are a great way to learn the skills required to make larger or more complex designs.

For years I have explored Eight-Pointed Star designs and related patterns. Typically, while I am creating one quilt, inspiration for numerous additional quilts will strike, resulting in a *series* of Eight-Pointed Star designs and diamond quilts. The patterns in this book are based on those same traditional block designs, but made in a *larger scale*.

The skill required to create detailed geometric patterns with diamonds and set-in seams can be daunting. This book is intended to introduce the shapes and techniques in a much easier format. Many of the quilts are made with just one block. Artists who are new to quiltmaking will enjoy this light-hearted pattern collection featuring larger shapes and fresh fabric combinations. Seasoned quiltmakers will enjoy the attractive designs that piece together in a relatively short time.

The basis for the designs in this collection is the 45° diamond, or parallelogram. This shape has two opposing parallel edges, and all four sides are of equal length. It differs from its "half-square" or right-angle counterpart, whose four sides are not equal. The designs created from the true diamond are more appealing to me than those created from right-angle triangles.

A 45° diamond or parallelogram (left) compared to a half-square "diamond" unit (right)

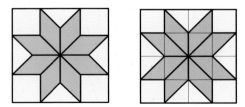

An Eight-Pointed Star made from true 45° diamonds (left) and similar Eight-Pointed Star made with right triangles or half-square triangles (right)

Versatile 45° diamonds are used in a variety of patterns. Traditional Starburst quilts are one-patch designs made up of diamonds. If you cut the diamond shapes in half or in quarters with additional seams, you create a myriad of new design possibilities. Other piecing options provide unlimited variations.

One-patch Starburst design

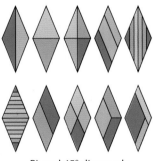

Pieced 45° diamonds

Another way to dramatically alter the appearance of the basic shape is to carefully cut the diamonds to feature prominent fabric motifs; this is known as *fussy cutting*.

When creating my own star designs, I find it easiest to cut perfect diamonds with my acrylic ruler designed specifically for that purpose. Two different sets of diamond rotary-cutting rulers are available from C&T Publishing for easy measurement and cutting. (See Resources, page 111.)

The patterns in this book provide materials lists and assembly directions for making easy quilts with the fast2cut® 45° diamond rulers or with traditional templates that you can make yourself from the template patterns provided, pages 107–110. I know you will enjoy the wide range of attractive, quick, star quilt patterns and will be inspired by the exciting designs of quilt artists in the Star Gallery, pages 35–52. Have fun making the quilts, and share your talents and creativity with those you love!

Happy Stitching!

Fabric Selection

Your fabric selection has a great influence on the project's appearance. This obvious statement has deeper meaning!

The quilt projects in this book feature large shapes and pieces, requiring minimal cutting and piecing. Selecting quiet, calm, solid, or tone-on-tone fabrics will result in a very large graphic design with *low visual interest*—in other words: *a boring quilt.* The surface will have little of the visual energy that a patterned fabric will provide.

Enhance the quilt design with changes in value (lightness to darkness), texture, and contrast. Adding small bits of unexpected colors will provide excitement and interest to a calm fabric collection.

Focus Fabrics

Fabrics with medium- and large-scale pattern designs provide the themes for the projects in this book. These are the "stars" of the projects; the larger the print or pattern scale, the more dramatic the design will be! Select one large-scale print as the theme or focus fabric. Determine the placement for this fabric in your project. You may need to *fussy cut* or select certain motifs from the print. Position the ruler over that motif and cut out single elements for the project.

A fabric collection with calm, solid, and tone-on-tone designs. Add an unexpected contrasting color for interest.

Jan's Tip

Be sure to purchase adequate yardage when selecting a fabric with large-scale designs. Quilt borders and fussy-cut, identical motifs require more yardage than allover patterns. I typically purchase 4–6 yards of any large-scale print when I have no specific project in mind. I purchase more yardage if the fabric is suitable for a large project. Remember: fabric designs are printed in limited quantity, they sell out rapidly, and they are rarely reprinted.

Examples of large-scale "focus" fabrics

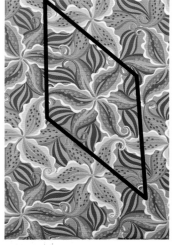

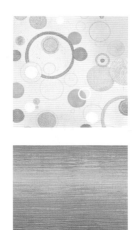

Select additional fabrics that coordinate with the large-scale focus fabric—fabrics with smaller print scales, different patterns or textures, and varying colors. Include a surprise color in a small quantity for interest and excitement. Use these bright surprise colors, sometimes called *zingers*, in limited quantities. If the project fabrics do not include any zingers, you can add narrow trim in a contrasting color to add interest or define a design area.

Fussy cut specific motifs from focus fabric.

Narrow, bright-colored trim enhances and defines the diamond edges.

Stripes and Geometrics

These two fabric styles provide line and texture within the design and can be used effectively to add design interest. The patterns may be printed, dyed, or even created by sewing several strips together to create a strip set.

Using an interesting, large-scale stripe within large shapes is very exciting! The fabric can be cut so that the stripe parallels an outer edge, creating a border, or so that the stripe bisects the shape in various ways.

Interesting Calm Fabrics

This category of fabrics supports the focus fabric. When viewed from a distance, the subtle pattern or lower contrast within the fabric complements the focus fabric. Calm fabrics, such as tone-on-tone blenders and monochromatic prints (prints with several shades and tints of just one color), provide a resting place for the eye and frequently create a cohesive background behind the focus fabric.

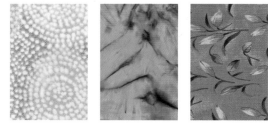

Interesting, calm fabric prints

Large-scale printed and dyed stripes

Striped fabrics incorporated within the diamonds,
setting pieces, and borders of several quilts

Smaller-scale, subtle stripes can also serve as calm fabrics, creating a contrast to a large-scale focus fabric, or can be used as narrow trim strips to enhance and visually separate two design areas.

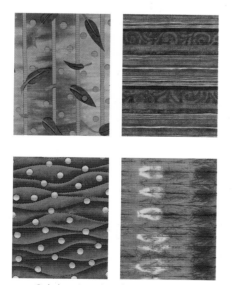

Subtle printed and woven stripes

Examples of subtle stripes in the details of various quilts

Geometric designs include any patterns that are regular repeats of lines, squares, triangles, stars, circles, dots, checks, and so on. The designs provide visual activity or *filling* for the quilt, and are companions to the focus fabric and the interesting calm fabrics.

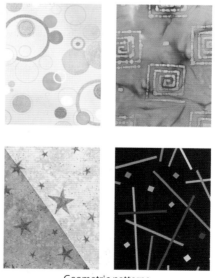

Geometric patterns

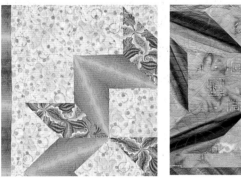

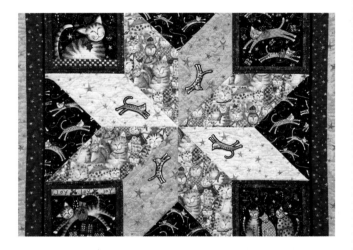

Examples of geometric patterns within the pieced
designs of various quilts

Prewashing Guidelines

Today's cotton fabrics, purchased from a reputable quilt shop, are high-quality, medium-weight cotton, with a good tight weave. I frequently sew my projects using unwashed yardage with excellent results. Fabrics purchased from discount stores or large chain stores may vary in quality.

In the past, fabrics often had a tendency to shrink significantly and lose excess dye when washed the first time. It was a common practice to prewash all fabrics prior to using them. It is still advisable to prewash with the following fabric types:

- Handwoven fabrics such as a madras plaid, Guatemalan stripes, or other ethnic fabric that you know to be hand-woven or hand-printed.

- Loosely woven fabrics such as homespun, some flannels, plaids, and brocade.

- Hand-dyed fabrics or batiks, especially supersaturated colors (anything medium to dark in value).

- Any blend or specialty fabric that you are unfamiliar with. If you do not know how it will appear or behave after laundering, wash to find out before using it in your quilt.

Laundering will remove the factory finishes applied to the fabric. When washing fabrics that have been dyed (such as hand-dyed, batik, tie-dyed or shibori), add a color stabilizer such as Synthrapol, Retayne, or Dharma Dye Fixative. Another option is to add a product designed to absorb excess dye molecules in the water, such as Shout Color Catcher, Woolite Dye Magnet, or Zero Dye Magnet (Canada). For more information, see Resources, page 111.

Typically, the fabric will require light pressing after laundering to smooth the wrinkles. An optional light mist of starch or fabric finish will add body to limp fabrics. If you use starch, add it just before working with the fabrics, and wash the project immediately after construction to avoid attracting insects that are attracted to starch. I do not recommend storing yardage that contains starch.

Jan's Tip

Evaluate your fabrics, and if you are in doubt, I suggest prewashing them before cutting them for your project.

Tools and Equipment

Sewing Equipment

SEWING MACHINE

- Straight stitch (suitable for seams in patchwork)
- Multiple stitches (if you are planning to do machine appliqué)

SEWING MACHINE ACCESSORIES

- Single-hole throat plate (provides a better stitch quality, particularly when sewing seams at the narrow tips of diamonds)
- Zigzag throat plate (for decorative stitching)
- Quarter-inch foot (to achieve accurate seam width)
- Open-toe appliqué foot (for any pattern with appliqué)
- Walking foot (may be necessary for piecing on bias edges)

Cutting Equipment

- Sharp sewing scissors or dressmaker's shears
- Rotary cutter with sharp blade

- Large or oversized cutting mat
- Several acrylic rulers designed for rotary cutting. I advise using products by the same manufacturer if possible.
- fast2cut® Fussy Cutter™ 45° diamond guide 6½″ ruler
- fast2cut® Fussy Cutter™ 45° diamond guide 3″ ruler
- Templates from stiff template plastic (optional)
- 6½″ × 24″ ruler
- Triangle ruler
- Large quilter's square (12″ × 12″ or larger)
- Omnigrid Invisi-Grip (optional)
- Sandpaper dots (optional)

DIAMOND RULERS

fast2cut® Fussy Cutter™ 45° Diamond Guide rulers: 6½″ × 6½″ and 3″ × 3″.

fast2cut® Half- & Quarter-Diamond Ruler Set

Sewing Notions

- Thread snips
- Seam ripper
- Sewing awl or stiletto
- Extra fine (silk-weight) glass-headed pins for precision pinning

- Sharp (not universal or ball point) sewing machine needles, size 10 or 12 (70 or 80), designed for sewing seams in woven fabrics
- Medium to heavyweight template plastic (optional)
- Pencil and permanent marking pen
- Isopropyl alcohol pads, in foil packaging, to remove ink from rulers

Pressing Equipment

- Iron
- Ironing board
- Spray starch or fabric finish
- Pump spray water bottle
- Distilled water (optional)

Use a steam iron that functions with or without water, allowing different types of pressing. Always *press* the fabric in an up-and-down motion to prevent stretching or distorting.

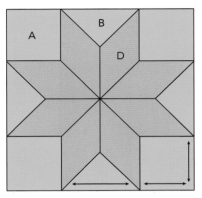

Eight-Pointed Star; A = corner square,
B = setting triangle, D = diamond

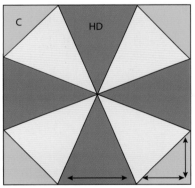

Kaleidoscope; HD = half-diamond;
C = corner triangle

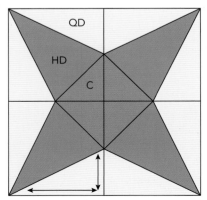

Rocky Road to Kansas; HD = half-diamond;
QD = quarter-diamond; C = corner triangle

Cutting Techniques

Geometric Components: 45° Diamonds, Quarter-Diamonds, and Half-Diamonds

The patterns in this book use several different sets of rulers designed specifically for cutting diamonds. (See Diamond Rulers, page 9.) The rulers are designed for easy measurement and rotary cutting. If you prefer, you may create plastic templates for tracing the shapes onto the fabric to cut with scissors. (Template patterns begin on page 107.) A big advantage of the diamond rulers is the ability to safely rotary cut against them.

The two sizes of diamonds used throughout this book are referred to by their unfinished size: 6½″ and 3″. That is the distance from one parallel side to the other. The finished sizes of the diamonds are 6″ and 2½″. If you want to cut diamonds from strips, cut 6½″ strips for the larger diamonds and 3″ strips for the smaller diamonds.

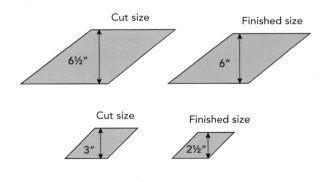

Companion Geometric Shapes: Squares and Right Triangles

The "stars of the show" are 45° diamonds, but you will need companion shapes in order to create myriad patterns. Playing with the placement of the shapes will yield interesting variations. The most common companion shapes are squares and triangles. To the left and on the following page are the shapes and companion shapes used for the quilts in this book. Arrows in the diagram indicate straight grain.

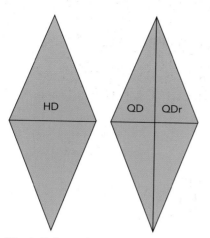

HD = half-diamond; QD = quarter-diamond;
QDr = quarter-diamond reversed

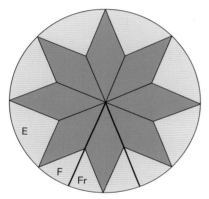

Star-in-a-Circle; E = quarter circle;
F, Fr = eighth circle and eighth circle reversed

Cutting with Scissors

1. Trace around the diamond or partial diamond template or ruler with a pencil or extra fine permanent pen.

2. Cut along the lines with sewing scissors. Cut directly **on** the drawn line or just **inside** the line to avoid making the shapes larger than they should be.

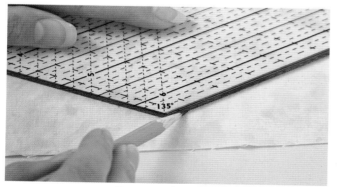

Trace around template

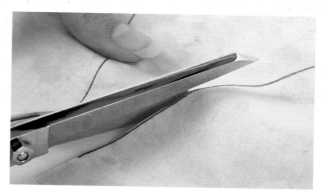

Cut out shapes, trimming just inside pencil line.

Rotary Cutting

When rotary cutting, I recommend that you use one of the products below to help your ruler grip the fabric and prevent slipping.

- **Invisi-Grip.** Cut the film slightly smaller than your ruler size. Place it on the underside of your ruler

- **Adhesive-backed sandpaper dots.** Cut each dot in half. Adhere the half dots to the ruler bottom on each tip and edge to add stability.

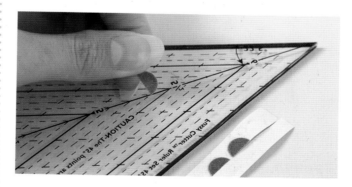

- **Steam-a-Seam 2 or Steam-a-Seam Lite.** Cut a narrow strip or two, and remove the paper backing. Center the strip on the ruler bottom, and adhere it by simply pressing it with your hand; the pebbly, slightly sticky surface will provide stability.

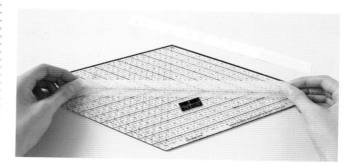

STRIP METHOD

This is the simplest method. Use it when you want several diamonds cut from the same fabric without regard to motifs or designs. Diamonds cut this way will have 2 straight-grain edges and 2 bias edges.

1. Cut 6½″ strips for the larger diamond and 3″ strips for the smaller diamond.

2. Open the strips so they are not folded; layer 2 or 3 strips right side up, if desired. Align the sides of the diamond ruler with the edges of the strip and cut along the diagonal ends. Continue cutting across the strip until you have the number of diamonds you need.

   - One fabric strip 6½″ × 42″ (cut selvage to selvage) will yield 4 or 5 diamonds.

   - One fabric strip 3″ × 42″ (cut selvage to selvage) will yield 12 or 13 diamonds.

CUT-AND-ROTATE METHOD

1. Place a full or partial diamond ruler on the fabric. The fabric may be single or multiple layers, but I suggest no more than 4 layers for accurate cutting. Cut around the edge(s) on the *far side of the ruler away from your body* with a rotary cutter.

2. Rotate the shape on the cutting mat or rotate the mat to comfortably cut the remaining edges. A turntable-style cutting mat is nice for cutting smaller diamonds.

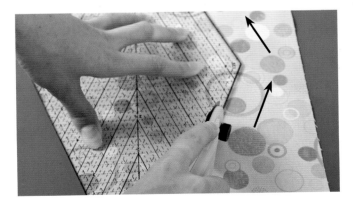

BUDDY RULER TECHNIQUE

1. Position the diamond ruler (or partial diamond ruler) on the fabric. Cut around the edge(s) on the *far side of the ruler away from your body* with a rotary cutter as shown in Step 1, at left.

2. Align a second "buddy ruler" along the *forward edge* of the shape being cut. Hold securely in place and carefully slide the diamond ruler aside slightly. *Cut against the buddy ruler.* Realign the diamond ruler with the cut edges and repeat the process with the buddy ruler to cut the remaining edge. Do not inadvertently cut into the diamond shape.

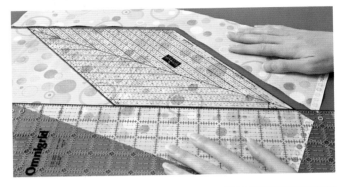

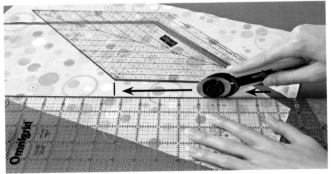

FUSSY CUTTING MOTIFS

1. Position the large diamond ruler over a motif in the fabric.

2. Trace the key design elements onto the ruler with a permanent pen, such as a Sharpie or Identipen. The marks are easily removed later with rubbing alcohol or a plastic eraser.

3. After you have cut the first diamond, use the markings on the ruler to help you correctly position the ruler on the printed fabric so you can fussy cut additional diamonds. You can cut 8 of one image, or combinations such as 4 of one image and 4 of a companion image.

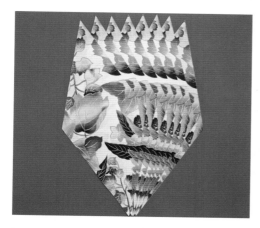

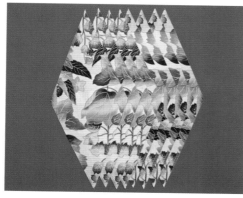

CUTTING DIAMONDS FROM STRIPES

Cutting with the Template

1. Working with striped fabric or a pieced strip set, layer the fabric wrong sides together with the stripes aligned.

2. Align a long straight ruler (6½″ × 24″ or 6″ × 24″) with a stripe or seamline. Cut strips 3″ or 6½″ wide, the **same width** as the diamond template you plan to use.

3. Align the diamond template with the cut edges of the fabric strip. Cut diamonds from the fabric strips.

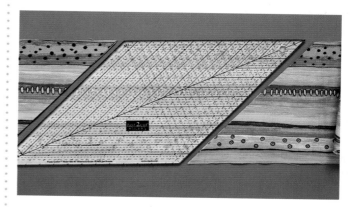

Cutting with the Straight Ruler

1. Follow Steps 1 and 2 above. Then rotate the long straight ruler, aligning the 45° guide at the cut edge of the strip.

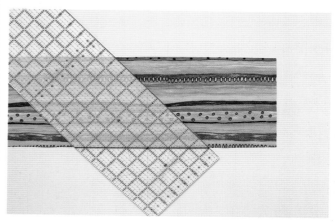

2. Cut the diamonds the *same width* as the strips. Watch the grainline of the diamond shape. Two edges should be parallel with the stripe, on the straight grain; 2 edges should be true 45° bias.

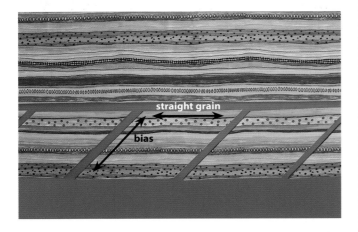

CUTTING HALF DIAMONDS

Option 1

Cut full diamond shapes, then subcut the diamond in half horizontally through all layers, creating half diamonds. *Note*: when you sew 2 of these half diamonds together, they will be smaller than those cut using the original 6½″ or 3″ diamond, due to the center seam allowance.

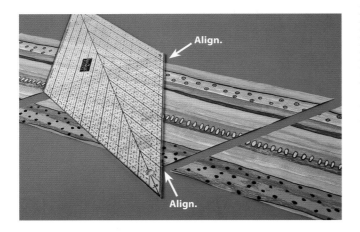

Option 2

Use the 6 ½″ half-diamond template pattern, page 109 (See Resources, page 111.). Layer fabric with wrong sides together to cut mirror-image pieces. Align the ruler edge with the strip edge. Cut half-diamonds, rotating the ruler for alternating cuts.

Half-diamond shapes cut from layered fabric have mirror-image patterns.

Jan's Tip

A benefit of using a half-diamond ruler is that a seam allowance has been added to the ruler. When you sew together 2 half-diamonds cut from a fast2cut® half-diamond ruler, you will produce a full-size diamond that will match whole diamonds cut from the 3″ or 6½″ diamond rulers.

Creating Easy Split Diamonds

DIAMONDS SPLIT LENGTHWISE

1. Cut 2 different fabric strips 4¼˝ wide for the 6½˝ diamond; cut 2 strips 2½˝ wide for the 3˝ diamond.

2. Place the strips right sides together; sew together along 1 long edge. Press the seam open.

3. Lay the diamond ruler on the strip set, aligning the *lengthwise* center line of the ruler with the seam. Cut diamonds 1 at a time from the pieced strips; do not overcut into the surrounding fabric.

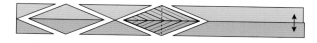

4. Remove the stitching from the remainder of the seam (of strip set).

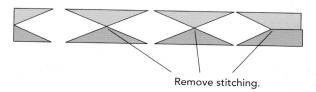

Remove stitching.

5. Place the fabric right sides together once again; sew the remaining long edge together. Press the seam open. Cut 2 (6½˝) or 4 (3˝) diamonds from this combination.

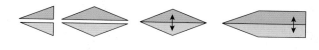

- Two strips 4¼˝ × 42˝ sewn together typically yield *4 split 6½˝ diamonds.*

- Two strips 2½˝ × 42˝ sewn together typically yield *8 split 3˝ diamonds.*

DIAMONDS SPLIT CROSSWISE

1. Cut 2 different fabric strips 9½˝ wide for the 6½˝ diamond; cut 2 strips 5˝ wide for the 3˝ diamond.

2. Place the strips right sides together; sew together along 1 long edge. Press the seam open.

3. Lay the diamond ruler on the fabric, aligning the *crosswise* centerline of the ruler with the seam. Cut diamonds 1 at a time from the pieced strips—do not overcut into the surrounding fabric.

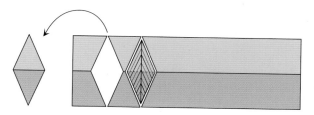

4. Remove the stitching from the remainder of the seam. (See Step 4, Diamonds Split Lengthwise, above.)

5. Place the fabric right sides together once again; sew the remaining long edge together. Press the seam open. Cut diamonds from this combination.

- Two strips 9½˝ × 42˝ (cut selvage to selvage) typically yield *9–10 split 6½˝ diamonds.*

- Two strips 2½˝ × 42˝ (cut selvage to selvage) typically yield *16–17 split 3˝ diamonds.*

Construction Techniques

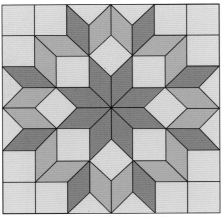

Eight-Pointed Star or LeMoyne Star

Many of the quilt designs in this book are constructed in the same fashion. These general instructions will apply to the majority of the patterns, with additional details included as needed with the instructions for each specific project.

Blocks such as the Eight-Pointed Star, Broken Star, Kaleidoscope, Harbor Lights, Maltese Cross, and others are *radial* designs with 45° angled seams crossing through a central axis. Radial designs require more accuracy than those based on squares and rectangles.

Surrounding the diamonds or half-diamonds in each of the designs are the companion geometric shapes—primarily squares, triangles, and quarter or eighth circles. Assembling many of these blocks requires sewing seams along the side of each shape and then backstitching or back tacking ¼″ away from each end. This technique is known as "setting-in" a seam, mitering a corner, or sewing Y seams.

Some of the blocks can be simplified to enable construction without set-in seams. This will result in additional seams within a block, but the ease of sewing may be worth the trade-off. Special fabrics are better set-in; a seam would fracture the fabric print.

Jan's Tip

Pretrimming the narrow points, or tips, of the diamonds often helps to align block pieces accurately. When applicable, the patterns include pretrimming instructions for points to simplify alignment when piecing blocks together.

Broken Star or Carpenter's Wheel

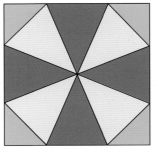

Kaleidoscope

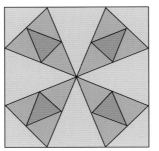

Harbor Lights

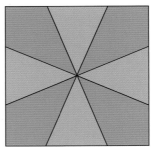

Maltese Cross

Accuracy First

An accurate ¼˝ seam is essential for making any quilt, but it is even more important when sewing Eight-Pointed Stars and other blocks made from diamonds.

- For best results, use a single-hole throat plate and a quarter-inch presser foot on your sewing machine.

Standard throat plate (left); single-hole throat plate (right)

Examples of quarter-inch presser feet

- Use a **sharp** machine needle (not universal or ball point). Set the stitch length to 1.5 or 2mm (12 to 15 stitches per inch).

- Calibrate your seam allowance width **before** sewing your project! Accurate seam allowances are **critical to the success of your quilt.**

TEST FOR ACCURACY

1. Sew a seam test: Cut a 1½˝ wide strip of fabric. Subcut into 6–9 sections.

2. Sew 3 pieces together along the long edges.

3. Press the seams **open.**

4. Measure the total width of the 3-strip sample. It should measure 3½˝. If the strip sample is wider than 3½˝, you need to **make your seam 1 thread wider.** If the strip sample is narrower than 3½˝, you need to **make your seam 1 thread narrower.**

Jan's Tip

A handy tool is available to help you obtain an exact scant ¼˝ seam allowance—the Perfect Piecing Seam Guide (See Resources, page 111). Lower the needle into the hole and lower the presser foot, keeping the tool perpendicular to the presser foot. Observe the right edge of the tool. Where is the perfect edge in relationship to your presser foot? For greater accuracy, create a raised guide on your machine bed, referring to Step 5, below.

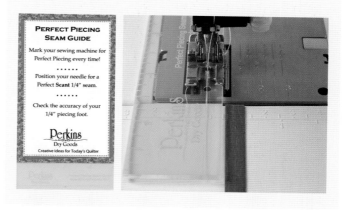

5. Once you have an accurate seam allowance, make a guide on your machine just ahead of and to the right of the presser foot. A guide can consist of any of the following:

- Fine, permanent ink line on the bed of your machine.
- Stack of blue painter's tape
- Adhesive-backed moleskin or dense foam (sold in the foot-care section of the pharmacy)
- Commercial guide available on some sewing machines

Pressing Matters

Each of the quilt projects includes pressing instructions. For greatest accuracy, press each seam after sewing it. Many of the assembly and quilt diagrams include pressing arrows for your convenience. Single-headed arrows indicate seams pressed to the side; double-headed arrows indicate seams pressed open.

- If your seams are to be pressed **open**, press from the wrong side, then inspect on the front.
- If your seams are to be pressed **to the side**, press from the front, then inspect on the back.
- Use your iron's **shot-of-steam** feature to flatten fabrics.

● Use a mist of water before pressing if you do not have a shot-of-steam feature.

● Use a light mist of *spray starch* or *fabric finish* to provide body and prevent stretching of bias edges.

● After the quilt is assembled, press with steam to flatten, smooth, and straighten the quilt top.

● Inspect seams from the wrong side, pressing all seams consistently in the same direction. Correct any seams that have accidentally twisted in the wrong direction, as this will be visible from the front of the quilt and may potentially affect the machine quilting results at the seam.

Jan's Tip

Watch for pleats or folds at the seam when pressing. If the seam is not fully pressed, it changes the dimension of the quilt unit.

Mastering the Eight-Pointed Intersection

A beautifully matched intersection is the hallmark of a skilled quilter. I use two different methods for obtaining accurately matching centers: pressing the seams to one side and pressing seams open. For either method, follow these tips for success:

● Be sure that your cutting is accurate and that all 8 pieces have true 45° angles at the center point.

● Mark the ¼˝ seamline intersections at the points and corners, if desired, to help with matching up and backstitching.

● Press seam allowances carefully to control them and distribute bulk neatly.

● Avoid excessive ironing on the right side over the raised seams in the center; this creates a "cooked" or shiny effect on the fabric.

● Maintain an accurate seam allowance all the way through the construction.

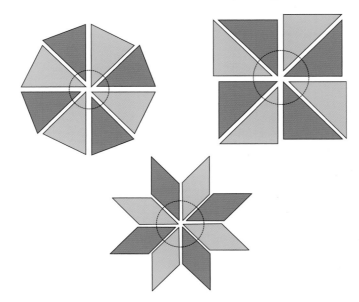

METHOD ONE:
SEAMS PRESSED TO THE SIDE

1. Join pairs of units together (diamonds, half-diamonds, or right triangles) using an accurate ¼˝ seam. Keep the same color on top (if colors alternate), and sew from the same direction for each of the 4 pairs. For diamonds that will have set-in seams, end your stitching at the ¼˝ seam and backstitch.

2. Press the seam *to the same side* on all 4 pairs.

3. Trim the points at a 90° angle, as shown, to create a tidy corner and eliminate extra fabric.

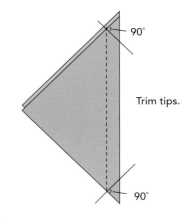

Right triangles: sew from edge to edge and trim the points.

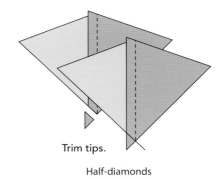

Half-diamonds

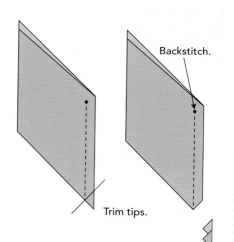

Backstitch.

Trim tips.

Diamonds: backstitch at the top of the seam, and trim the inner point.

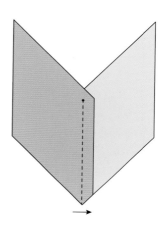

4. Align the points and seams between 2 pairs of units. Secure with a fine silk-weight pin.

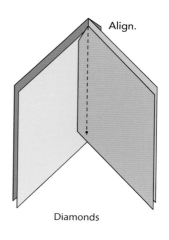

Align.

Diamonds

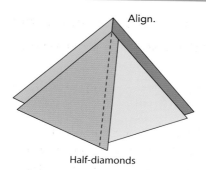

Align.

Half-diamonds

5. For diamonds, sew 2 pairs together, backstitching at the ¼″ seamline at each end. For half-diamonds, begin sewing at either end, backstitching only at the sewn ¼″ seam. Press the seam in the same direction as the previous seams.

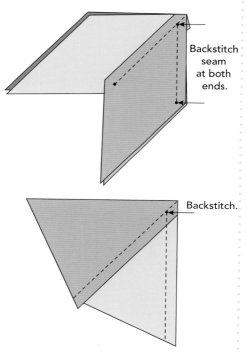

Backstitch seam at both ends.

Backstitch.

6. Repeat Steps 4 and 5 with the remaining units to make 2 half blocks, each containing 4 diamonds or half-diamonds. Press the seams in the same direction.

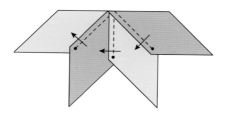

7. Align the 2 halves, matching the center seams. Secure with a fine silk-weight pin.

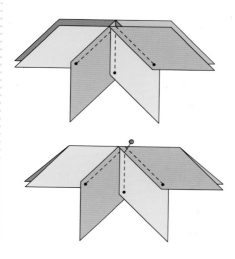

8. Sew about 5 stitches across the center intersection. Open and check the alignment. Carefully rip out the stitches, and try again if it doesn't meet properly.

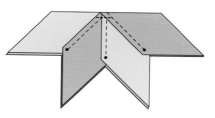

9. When you are satisfied with the alignment, sew the center seam, backstitching at the ¼″ seamline at both ends for diamonds. Sew edge to edge for other shapes.

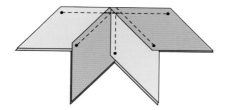

10. Press the center seam in the direction established by previous seams. The seams at the center will flip open, as shown. Press with steam from the wrong side to flatten the center intersection.

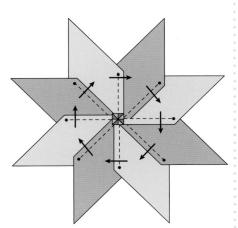

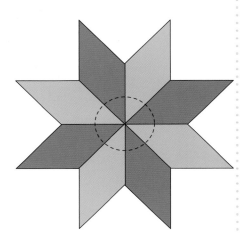

Jan's Tip

Pressing seams to the side will always result in slightly offset spiraling seams in the center, due to the distribution of seams at the center point.

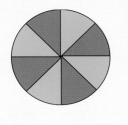

METHOD TWO:
SEAMS PRESSED OPEN

This method is very similar to the previous technique but, when properly executed, results in a perfectly aligned center point. As always, *maintain consistent seam allowances* during construction and press seams open carefully for success. A diamond is used in the illustrations, but the process is the same for other shapes.

1. Join pairs of units together (diamonds, half-diamond triangles, or right triangles). Keep the same color on top (if colors alternate), and sew from the same direction for each of the 4 pairs. For diamonds that will have set-in seams, backstitch at the ¼" seamline.

2. Press the seam *open* on all 4 pairs. Trim the tips, creating a tidy 90° square corner.

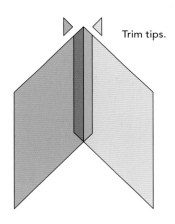

Trim tips.

3. Align the seams between 2 pairs of units. Secure with a pin.

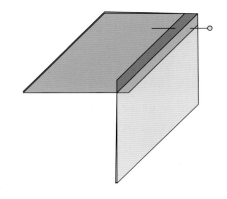

4. Sew 2 pairs together, sewing all the way through the seam allowances in the center. For diamonds, stop sewing and backstitch at the ¼" seamline at the end. Press the seams open.

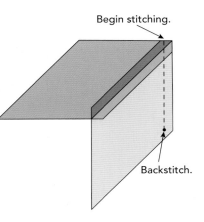

Begin stitching.

Backstitch.

5. Repeat Steps 3 and 4 with the remaining units to make half blocks.

6. Align 2 half blocks right sides together, matching the center seams. Secure with a fine silk-weight pin.

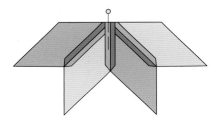

7. Sew about 5 stitches across the center intersection. Open and check for alignment.

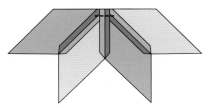

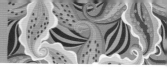

8. Once you are satisfied with the alignment, sew the center seam, backstitching at the ¼˝ seamline at each end for diamonds. Sew edge to edge for other shapes. Press the center seam open; press with steam from the wrong side to flatten the center intersection.

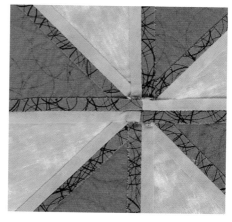

Jan's Tip

The match at the center of the eight points is more easily achieved when the seams are pressed open.

Star Construction

The quilt projects in this book include star blocks constructed with and without set-in seams. Often your fabric will dictate which method to use. If it doesn't matter whether it has a seam or not, you can choose the easier method without set-in seams. Either way, it's not too difficult, and I've included plenty of tips and helpful hints to guarantee success with just a little practice.

For either method, cut all the components for the quilt pattern as directed, and then arrange the pieces on a design wall to verify that you like the fabrics together before sewing.

Each project includes an assembly diagram and instructions indicating whether you set-in the seams or not.

- Stitch seams **edge to edge** when indicated by a straight line and no red dots.
- Stop seams at the ¼˝ seamline and backstitch 3 to 4 stitches where indicated by a red dot.

STARS WITHOUT SET-IN SEAMS

1. Study the exploded diagram included with the chosen quilt design. Identify the smallest components and how they are sewn together. Note which direction the seams are pressed. For the Eight-Pointed Star, the smaller triangles along the sides of the blocks (not the corners) will be sewn to the diamond first.

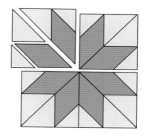

2. Position the first pieces to be sewn right sides together. The 45° points on triangles and diamonds will align.

3. Sew from edge to edge, beginning at the outer pointed end. If your sewing machine tends to distort or destroy the pointy tip of the diamond, try these tricks:

- Use a **thread catcher**, a small scrap of fabric that you sew onto at the beginning and end of each seam. When beginning the next seam, grasp the thread catcher, applying gentle pressure when sewing to encourage the fabric to feed smoothly at the start of the seam.
- Use a disposable paper **starter** such as a small adhesive-backed paper note. Lay the paper on your work surface with the adhesive side up. Place the pair of

fabric pieces on top of the paper as shown; the fabric on the bottom will stick lightly to the low-tack adhesive on the note. Sew through all layers. Tear the paper *toward the point* to remove.

Note: When using a smooth-bottomed presser foot, the tacky paper starter may cling to the foot. If that happens, adjust the fabric points to cover more of the paper.

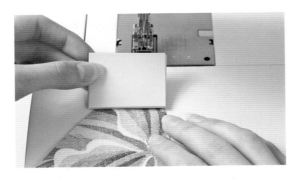

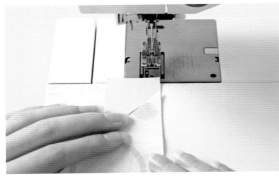

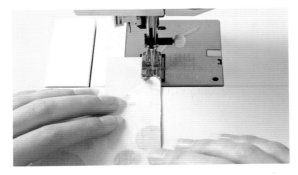

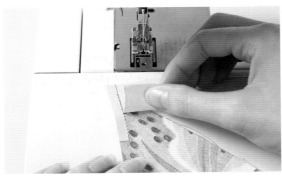

● For easier alignment, pretrim the tips before sewing. Use either of the fast2cut® 45° diamond rulers. Align the 2 fabric shapes right sides together. Position the ruler on top of both fabrics, aligning the ruler with the edges on either side of the point, as shown. Trim the tip. *Optional*: trim the tips on all of the remaining pieces at the same time.

Jan's Tip

For speed, sew all of the same units at the same time. Stack multiples of the same shape pieces and chain piece the units, sewing one pair right after the next in succession.

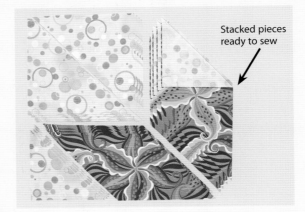

Stacked pieces ready to sew

4. Press the seams according to the pattern instructions. Seams may be pressed *open, to the side,* or a *combination of both methods* within the same quilt top. All units are pressed consistently in the same direction during construction unless directed otherwise.

5. Trim any dog-ears or fabric tips with scissors or a rotary cutter during construction to create tidy corners.

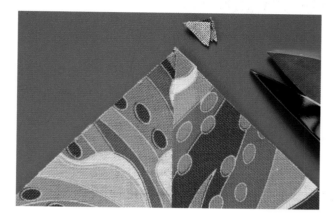

6. Add the next triangle to the first pair of pieces. Place the units right sides together, aligning the upper edge. Sew.

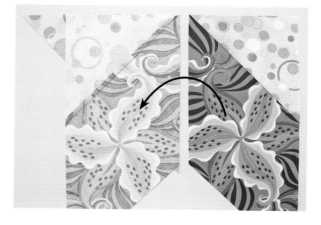

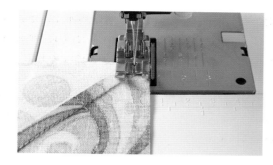

7. Press the seams in the same direction as the previous seams. Check the front to ensure seams are fully pressed without pleats or folds at the seamline.

8. Construct the mirror-image sections and any additional block units in the same manner to create one quarter of the block.

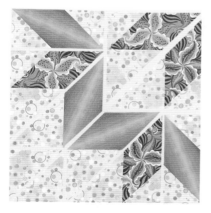

9. Sew the 4 block units together, pressing seams open or to one side as instructed, or as you prefer.

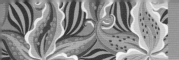

STARS WITH SET-IN SEAMS

1. Study the exploded diagram included with the chosen quilt design. Set-in seams are indicated by a red dot in the assembly diagram. Follow the steps in Mastering the Eight-Pointed Intersection, page 18, for either pressing seams to one side or pressing open to create the center of the star block. Mark the ¼″ seamline intersections at the points and corners, if desired, to help with matching up and backstitching.

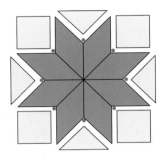

2. Set the triangles into the sides of the block first. Align and pin the short side of a triangle, right sides together, matching ¼″ marks with the edge of the corresponding diamond. Sew with the diamond on top, stitching from the raw edges of the outer point to the seam at the center; backstitch. You may need to fold the adjacent diamond back out of your way when sewing and move seam allowances aside as you approach the stopping point.

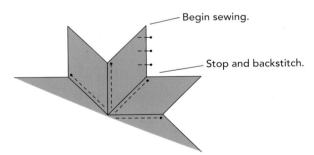

— Begin sewing.

— Stop and backstitch.

3. With the triangle on top, begin sewing at the outer raw edges. Sew toward the center and backstitch at the center seam. Align and pin the second short side of the triangle to the adjacent diamond. Press the seams toward the triangle. Repeat the process for each triangle.

4. Align and pin a square with the side of a diamond, right sides together, to set-in the corner pieces. Sew from the outer edge to the ¼″ seam and backstitch.

5. Align and pin the 2nd side of the square to the adjacent diamond. Sew as before, and backstitch at the center seam. Press the seams toward the square. Repeat the process for each square.

STARS IN CIRCLES

I appliqué circular stars onto a background, so no worries about having to do any curved piecing or set your star into a circle. LeMoyne Stars feature just simple wedge shapes; Broken Stars and Snow Crystals have additional sections, sewn in a similar sequence.

1. Cut wedge shapes using templates made from the pattern provided (page 110). This pattern includes extra fabric in the outer portion of the wedge to allow the star to "float." This gives some visual space surrounding the star and prevents the star points from being chopped off.

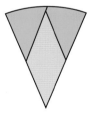

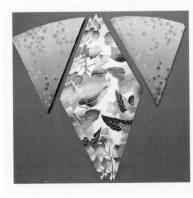

Jan's Tip

Lay out the diamond and wedge shapes before stitching. **Note:** *the wedge shapes are mirror images—there are 8 right and 8 left wedge pieces.*

Jan's Tip

For easy alignment, pretrim the tips with the small diamond ruler, as shown. The wedge fabric should intersect the diamond fabric at the ¼″ line of the ruler.

2. Sew all 8 of the wedge pieces to the corresponding edge of all 8 diamonds. Press seams toward the wedges.

3. Align a straight ruler with the adjacent raw edge of the diamond. Trim excess wedge fabric away as shown.

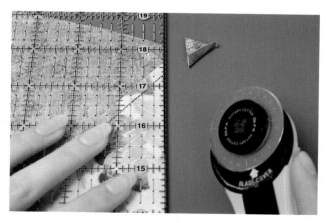

4. Sew the remaining 8 wedge shapes to the remaining side of the 8 diamonds. Press all seams away from the diamonds.

5. Pin 2 diamond units together, aligning seams. Sew the seam between the 2 units.

6. Press the seam *open* between the diamond units.

7. Trim the tips where 2 diamonds meet. Make 4 pairs.

8. Sew 2 pairs together to make a half star. Press the center seam open. Make 2 halves.

9. Align the center seams. Pin the center and machine sew about 5 stitches.

10. Check the intersection. When satisfied, sew edge to edge across the star.

11. Press the seam open.

12. Sew around the outer edge of the circular star with straight stitching, ¼″ from the raw edge, to stabilize it.

13. Press the seam allowance to the wrong side at the stitching line.

14. Fold the background fabric horizontally and vertically. Press the folds. Open and then fold diagonally in both directions. Press the folds.

15. Open the background square and position the circle on the background, matching the center of the circle with the center of the background. Rotate the circular center until the star points are oriented as you prefer. Pin securely all the way around the circle, keeping the circle centered and aligned with the pressed creases.

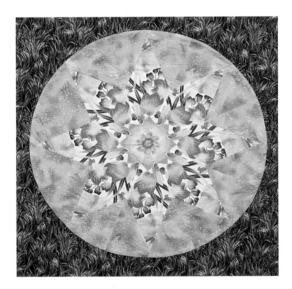

16. Change the presser foot and the throat plate on your machine to accommodate a wide zigzag stitch. Thread the machine with decorative thread, invisible thread, or a thread that matches either the circular wedge fabric or the square background fabric.

17. Set the machine to your preferred stitch pattern; sew around the circumference of the circle, stitching it to the background with invisible or decorative stitching.

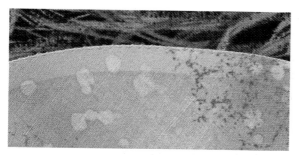

Narrow zigzag stitch

Machine buttonhole or blanket stitch

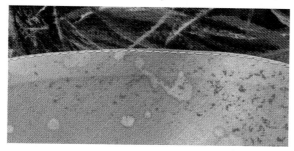

Straight stitch

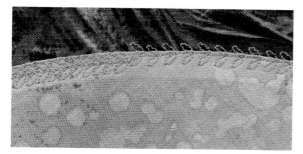

Decorative leaf stitch; two options for placement, centered over the edge or entire stitch on appliqué shape

Decorative star stitch

Finishing Stars in Circular Settings

1. Press the quilt top after the circle is appliquéd to the surface. If necessary, trim the background to straighten and square up the corners. You may leave the fabric behind the circle, or trim it away if desired.

2. To trim the background, carefully lift the fabric on the wrong side, separating the 2 layers. Snip through the background, creating a slit wide enough for the scissor tips.

3. Carefully trim inside the stitching line without cutting the front of the quilt, leaving at least a ¼″ seam allowance. Remove the center and use in a future project.

4. If desired, add borders to enhance and finish the quilt top.

Sizzling Embellishment: Adding a Sliver of Color

This is one of my favorite techniques—adding a dash of color along the edge of a design, providing contrast, definition, and sophisticated polish to any quilt. Many of my quilts feature narrow strips of fabric (¼″ wide finished) that outline a star or enhance borders with an exciting sizzle of color. Fabrics are deliberately bright, strong, or contrasting so that the tiny line of color will be visible.

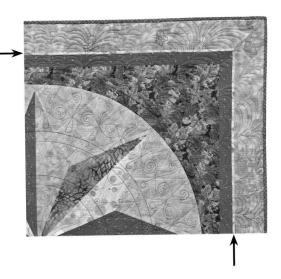

To add a slender strip of fabric at the edge of a diamond or border strip, cut several 1″ strips of fabric in a contrasting, bright accent color. You will need to sew these strips using a *½″ seam*. To make a guide, position a ruler beneath the presser foot.

- Lower the needle to **touch the right edge** of the ½″ mark.

- Lower the presser foot to hold the ruler in place.

- Observe the guides on the throat plate; are there any at the ½″ point? If so, use that as your guide when stitching.

- If your machine does not have a guide at ½″, position a thick, sticky piece of tape or moleskin to provide a sewing guide.

NARROW ACCENT TRIM APPLICATION

There are two methods for applying the narrow trim. The first option may be easier for beginners. The second option is also easy, but you must be able to judge a ¼″ distance by eye.

For either method, after the trim has been added, continue project construction, sewing components as usual. Keep the embellished strip or diamond on the **top surface** so you can see the embellishment stitching line on the wrong side of the fabric when sewing. The narrow strip will appear at the edge of the piece where it is attached.

Option 1

1. Place a 1″-wide embellishment strip *right sides together* with a diamond or border strip, aligning the raw edges. Stitch the 2 layers together with a ½″ seam using a 2.0 stitch length.

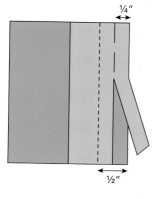

2. *Grade the seam:* trim ¼″ of the embellishment strip away *to the right of the stitching line,* reducing bulk in the seamline.

3. Fold the embellishment strip over, aligning the raw edges, and press. The narrow strip is now *sewn and pressed to the surface* of the larger piece; it is not a narrow border, and it does not increase the overall size of the original diamond or border strip.

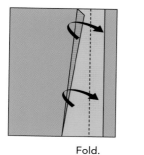

Fold. Press.

Option 2

1. Position the 1″ strip on top of the diamond or border, allowing ¼″ of the diamond or border to show at the right edge. Stitch the 2 layers together with a seam ½″ from the raw edge using a 2.0 stitch length.

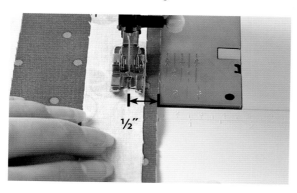

2. Press the embellishment strip neatly against the stitching line (hidden inside the fold).

3. Place the diamond or border strip right side down on a cutting mat. Trim away any embellishment extending beyond the outer edge with a rotary cutter.

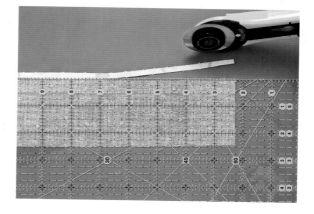

4. When adding trim to diamonds, cut away excess bulk created at the diamond tips. Trim only the interior seam allowance of the accent fabric, between the diamond point and the outer accent point.

Borders

The quilt patterns and gallery quilts in this book feature a variety of borders. While I have no particular border formula, I do have some favorite combinations.

- **Spacer strip border:** Add a narrow border 1″–3″ wide using fabric that matches the star background. This narrow border provides visual space between the central star and the borders or secondary pattern surrounding the center.

- **Double border:** Add 2 fabric strips of different widths.

- **Triple border:** Add 3 fabric strips of different widths.

- **Combination borders:** Add strips of varying widths, plus a narrow contrasting trim strip.

- **Bias-cut striped border:** Cut stripes on the bias. Add light-weight fusible interfacing to the back of the fabric before sewing to the quilt top for stability. Mitered corners are recommended.

- **Striped border:** Cut border strips perpendicular to the stripe for dramatic color effect.

- **Preprinted border strips:** Fabrics are specially printed in linear bands for borders.

Jan's Tip

*When possible, cut the borders parallel to the selvage **before** cutting the other components of the quilt. The lengthwise grain is the most stable and will minimize wavy or rippling borders. Typically, cutting lengthwise requires more yardage to create a continuous border. If you have less yardage to work with, or the printed pattern works better in sections, cut the border strips in shorter lengths, either lengthwise or cross grain, and sew the strips end to end. Use a walking foot to prevent stretching the upper layer of fabric when sewing the strips together.*

* **Do not add borders without measuring the quilt top first.** Always mark opposing borders, and pin the border to the top on a flat surface. This takes a few extra minutes, but it will ensure that the borders will fit the quilt top accurately, providing a polished finish without ruffling at the edge of the quilt.*

* Use a walking foot when sewing and adding borders to avoid stretching one or more of the layers.*

BORDERS WITH BUTTED CORNERS

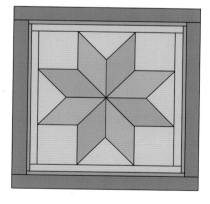

The simplest and most straightforward borders are applied directly to the quilt top—a border-as-you-go process. Work on a large, flat surface such as the dining room table or kitchen counter to keep the quilt top flat and straight. Use a dressmaker's measuring tape or a carpenter's retractable ruler.

1. Measure the length of the quilt top through the center and in several other places. (Do not use the outer side measurements, as the edges can be stretched from handling.) Find the average of these measurements and cut 2 side borders to this length.

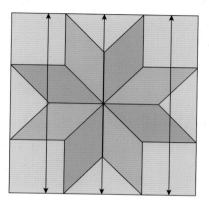

2. Fold both borders in half, bringing the short edges together to find the center. Mark each center fold with a pin or a light pencil mark.

3. Place the quilt top right side up on a flat, smooth surface. Place 1 border right side down along the quilt edge, matching center points. Pin in the center and at both ends. Pin approximately every 4″–5″ along the length. Pin the second border to the opposite side.

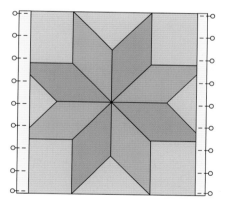

4. Sew the first 2 borders to the quilt top. Press the seams toward the border.

5. Measure the width of the quilt top through the center in several places, including the borders just added. Find the average of these measurements, and cut 2 strips of your border fabric this length for the top and bottom. Mark the center points as before and pin the border strips to the top and bottom of the quilt, matching the centers and ends. Sew and press seams toward the border.

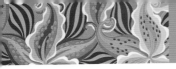
6. Continue adding borders in the same manner, measuring the quilt and cutting and adding borders until the quilt top reaches the desired size, or until the border width visually balances the quilt center. Press the seams outward for all borders.

MITERED BORDERS

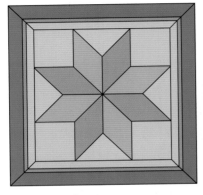

Mitered borders are attractive on star quilts because the angle at each corner is a 45° angle, echoing the angles within the quilt top. They are not difficult to sew when you know the secrets! Mitered borders are versatile and polished and may be used on any quilt style. When adding more than one border, sew the border strips together first and press; then add them to the quilt top as one unit. The project cutting instructions will tell you how long to cut the border strips.

1. Cut strips as directed, or as desired, to create the borders for your quilt. Audition the border strips by pinning them around your quilt top on the design wall and viewing the effect from a distance. The strips will be several inches wider and longer than the quilt. Note that the innermost borders do not need to be as long as the outer borders.

2. Once satisfied with the combination of the various fabrics and strip widths, sew the border strips together, matching the centers. Create four identical border units. Press the seams of the top and bottom border units *toward the outer border.* Press the seams of the side border units *toward the inner border.* This will allow the seams at the corners to butt together for easier matching when mitering the corners later. Skip this step if you are adding only 1 mitered border.

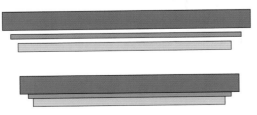

Make 4.

Cutting for Mitered Borders

To calculate the lengths to cut mitered borders for any quilt, follow these steps:

1. *Measure several places across the width of the quilt. Do not measure the outer edges, as they may have stretched. Find the average of these measurements, and write it down. Do the same for the length, and write the measurement down.*

2. *Measure the width of the border or border unit that you will be adding. Multiply this measurement by 2.*

3. *Add the result of Step 2 to the width and length from Step 1. Then add an extra 4˝. This is how long the border strips should be. You will need the extra length so that you can easily sew the diagonal seam at the corners.*

Formula:
Quilt width or length
+ (2 × border width)
+ 4˝
_____

Total = Length to cut borders

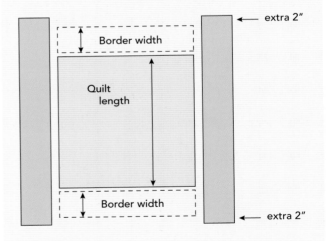

3. Fold each border to find the center. Mark it with a pin or a pencil mark. From the center, measure out *half* the width or length of the quilt and make a mark on each end. This is the point that you will align with the corner of the quilt top.

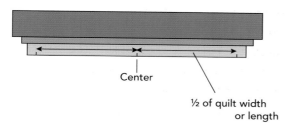

Center

½ of quilt width or length

4. Fold and mark the center point on all 4 edges of the quilt top with a pin or light pencil mark. Mark the end of the seam ¼˝ from the raw edge at all 4 corners.

5. Place the quilt top face up on a flat surface. Place 1 border on the quilt top, right sides together, aligning the inner border raw edges with the quilt top raw edges.

6. Align the center and end points; pin the border to the quilt top. Pin approximately 2˝–3˝ apart, easing fullness along the edges as necessary. Repeat on the opposing side, pinning the second border in place.

7. With the wrong side of the quilt on top, sew the border to the quilt top, beginning ¼˝ from the raw edge. Take 2 or 3 stitches, then backstitch to secure the end of the seam. Sew the seam, stopping and backstitching ¼˝ from the edge. Press the seams outward.

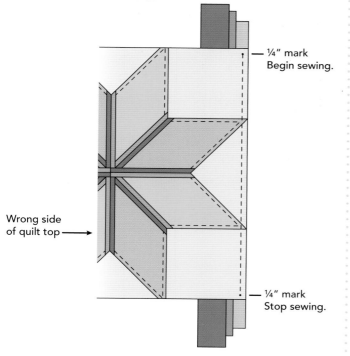

— ¼˝ mark
Begin sewing.

Wrong side of quilt top →

— ¼˝ mark
Stop sewing.

Jan's Tip

If your sewing table is small, extend the surface area by placing the ironing board next to the sewing table; adjust the board to a compatible height.

8. Repeat the process to sew the 2 remaining borders to the quilt top. The borders will extend beyond the quilt top at all of the corners.

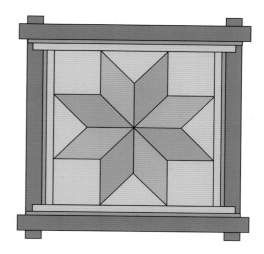

9. Fold the quilt diagonally, wrong sides together, aligning adjacent borders on top of each other. If necessary, fold back the pressed seam allowance, exposing the stitching line between quilt top and border.

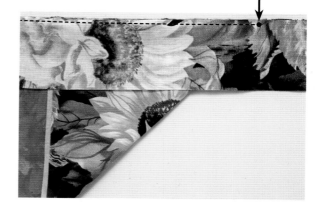

10. Position the fast2cut® 45° diamond ruler with one edge against the stitching line and the 135° corner at the end of the stitching line.

11. Mark the stitching line from the previous stitching to the outer edges of the border.

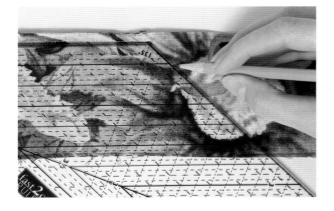

12. Pin the 2 border strips together along the marked line to hold them together for sewing. Sew the seam, beginning at the previous ¼˝ seam, backstitching and sewing to the outer edge of the border. Remove each pin as you sew. Backstitch.

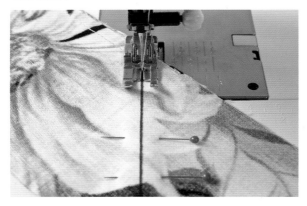

13. Open the quilt top. Press the corner neatly. Visually examine the corner to verify it lies perfectly flat without puckers or bulges. If necessary, adjust by removing and restitching the seam for a perfect corner.

14. Once satisfied with the seam, trim the excess border fabric, leaving a ¼˝ seam allowance. Repeat the process for all 4 corners and press the seams open.

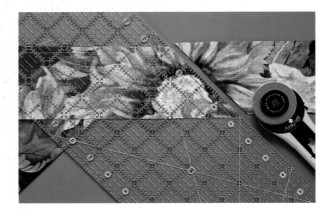

Finishing Notes

Once your quilt top is complete, you're ready to move on to layering, basting, quilting, and binding. There isn't space to cover all those details in this book. If you need additional information, check out some of the many good books on basic quiltmaking.

The backing yardage allows for a backing that is 6˝–8˝ larger than the quilt top. If you want to add a hanging sleeve that matches the backing, purchase an extra ¼–½ yard.

For these quick star quilts, I cut binding strips 2¾˝ wide. I like the look of a wider binding with the larger-scale blocks. Feel free to cut narrower binding strips if you prefer.

Star Gallery

Gleaming Cohorts, 57″ × 89″, 2003 by Jenny Bowker, Canberra, Australia

Play Stars Sweatshirt, LeMoyne Star variation,
2008 by Jacqueline Hand Lacey, Encinitas, CA

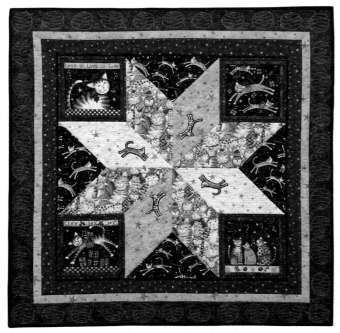

Christmas Kitties, Quick LeMoyne Star, 39½˝ × 39½˝, 2005 by Jan
Krentz; quilting by Lisa Taylor, Donegal, Ireland. One of three identical
quilts in the collections of Kim Farmer, Colorado Springs, CO; Dana
Stewart, Albuquerque, NM; and Lindsay Krentz, Long Beach, CA.

Star Search, Quick LeMoyne Star variation, 35½˝ × 35½˝, 2006
by S. Anne Sidell, Simi Valley, CA. From the collection of
Kathy Frye, Simi Valley, CA.

San Diego Star, Quick LeMoyne Star, 40″ × 40″, 2006 by Anna Mae Bach, San
Diego, CA; machine quilting by Linda Kamm, San Diego, CA

Caribbean Carnival, Original adaptation of a Rocky Road to Kansas design,
31″ × 31″, 2007 by Pat Wolfe, San Diego, CA

African Starlight, LeMoyne Star variation, 47½″ × 44½″, 2008
by Jacqueline Hand Lacey, Encinitas, CA

Quorn Star, Easy Rolling Star with borders, 54″ × 54″, 2007 by Christine Porter, Bristol, England

Chrysanthemum Starburst, String-Pieced Starburst variation, 101″ × 100″, 2007 by R. Lynne Lichtenstern, San Diego, CA; quilting by Susan Mezera, Poway, CA

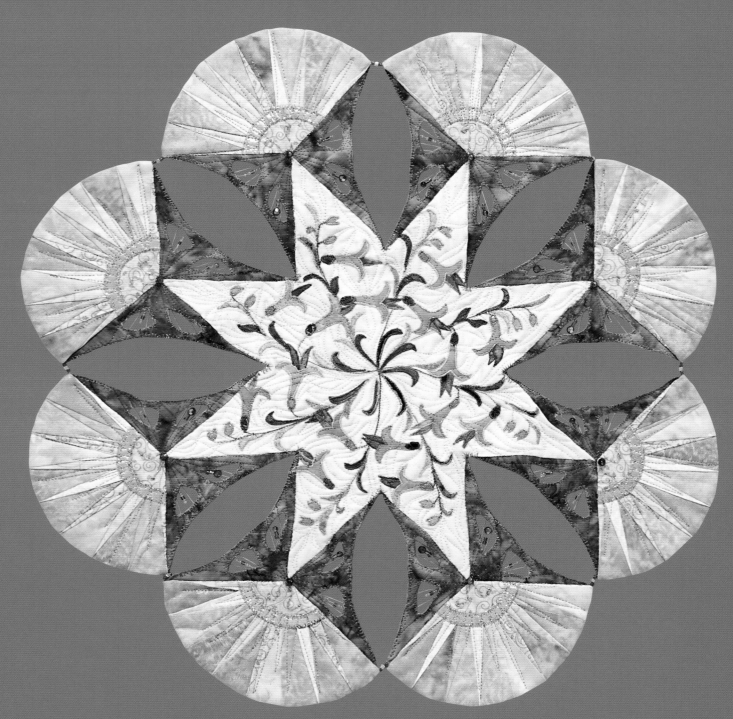

Star Flight, Original design of a LeMoyne Star variation with appliqué, cutwork, and beading embellishment, 20″ × 20″, 2008 by Patricia Votruba, San Diego, CA

My Sister's Garden, Kaleidoscope variation, 30″ × 30″, 2007
by Amy Wazny, San Diego, CA

Fuzzy Stars, LeMoyne Star variation, 44″ × 50″, 2007 by Kathy Butler, Philomath, OR

Tim's Star, LeMoyne Star variation, 38″ × 88″, 2007 by Amy Wazny, San Diego, CA; quilting by Marita Wallace, Santee, CA

Cottage Garden, Scrappy LeMoyne Star with border, 48″ × 48″, 2006
by J. Michelle Watts, Roswell, NM; quilted by Rita Galaska, Alto, NM

Hot Knights, Open Star, square-on-point setting, 55¼″ × 55¼″, 2007 piecing and quilting
by Marcia Harlamert, Palmer, AK; appliqué by Sarah Harlamert, Anchorage, AK

Romance, Open Star, 92˝ × 111˝, 2007, group quilt designed by Darlene C. Christopherson, China Springs, TX, and sewn by the members of her bee, the "Material Girls" in Waco, TX. (Bee members: Darlene C. Christopherson, Connie Watkins, Betteye R. Lewis, Patty Field, Ann M. Dyer, Jackie Lott, Colleen Barnes, Anita Selters, Susie Tatum.) quilting by Linda Buckner, Waco, TX

Tucson Memories, Broken Star, 29″ × 29″, 2007
by Rebecca Lighthill, San Marcos, CA

We Love the Ocean, Open Star, square-on-point setting,
42″ × 42″, 2007 by Betty Alofs, Lakeside, CA

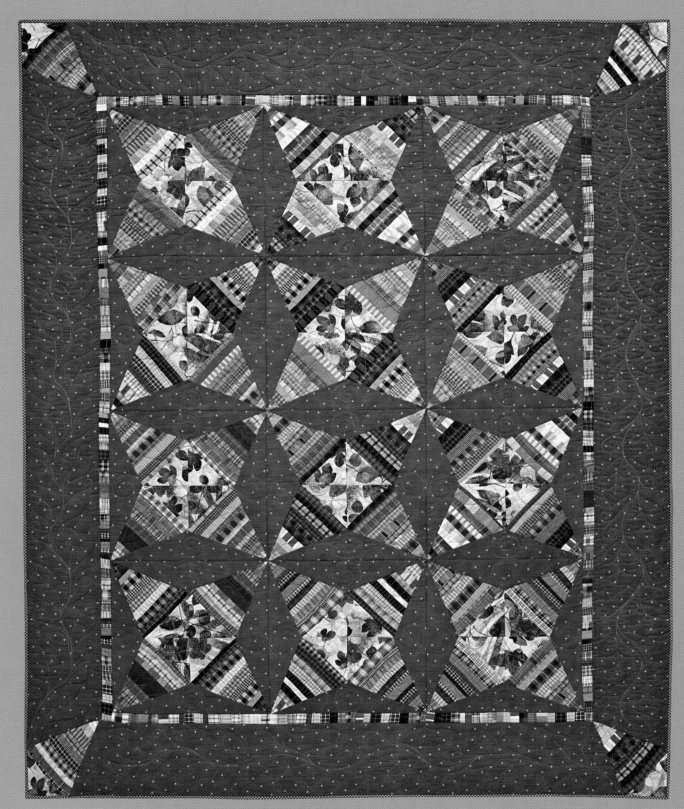

A Dozen Jacks, Rocky Road to Kansas variation, 65˝ × 81˝, 2007 by Pamela Kay, La Mesa, CA;
quilting by D'Andrea Mitchell, San Diego, CA

Bohemian Rhapsody, 68½″ × 68½″, 2007 by Jan Krentz; quilting
by D'Andrea Mitchell, San Diego, CA

Dream Catcher, Scrappy LeMoyne Star with border, 48″ × 48″, 2005
by J. Michelle Watts, Roswell, NM; quilting by Glenda Raby, Roswell, NM

Bug Party, LeMoyne Star variation, 62″ × 62″, 2007 by Mona Baran, Lake Havasu City, AZ; quilting by Ginny Clausen, Lake Havasu City, AZ

Alaskan Travel, 48″ × 48″, 2007 by Jan Krentz; quilting by Janet Sturdevant Stuart, Fort Worth, TX

Aloha, 39″ × 39″, 2007 by Jan Krentz; quilting by Janet Sturdevant Stuart, Fort Worth, TX

Free Spirit, Quick Rolling Star, 40½″ × 40½″, 2007 by Lorraine Marstall, San Diego, CA

Hot Pots Table Runner, LeMoyne Star variation, 18½˝ × 48˝,
2007 by Mona Baran, Lake Havasu City, AZ

Harbor Lights Table Runner, 15˝ × 45˝, 2007 by Jan Krentz

Tropical Currents, Rocky Road to Kansas variation, 65½″ × 81″, 2007 by Julia D. Zgliniec, Poway, CA; quilting by Laurie Daniells, Alpine, CA

The Eggs of the Rainbow Serpent, 54½″ × 70″, 2004 by Jenny Bowker, Canberra, Australia

Mandala, 58½″ × 58½″, 2003 by Jenny Bowker, Canberra, Australia

Flights of Fancy, Evening Star variation, 51″ × 65″, 2007 by Lorraine Marstall, San Diego, CA

Sunflower, 35″ × 35″, 2007 by Jan Krentz, quilting by D'Andrea Mitchell, San Diego, CA

Quick LeMoyne Star *without* set-in seams
fast2cut® Fussy Cutter™ 45° diamond ruler, 6½″
or 6½″ diamond template pattern, pages 107 and 108
Skill level: Easy
Block size: 29″ × 29″

AUTUMN LEAVES

41″ × 41″, 2007 by Jan Krentz; quilting by D'Andrea Mitchell, San Diego, CA

This quilt features a LeMoyne
Star with 8 identical diamonds,
each fussy cut from a gorgeous,
large-scale allover print. Create
the same effect for your quilt by
cutting 8 identical diamonds. For
a slightly different look, cut 2
sets of 4 identical diamonds, with
each set featuring a different
motif from the focus fabric.

YARDAGE	FOR	CUTTING
1 to 2 yards floral print*	Diamonds	Fussy cut 8 identical diamonds, 6½˝.
1¼ yards green floral print	Background	Cut 4 squares 9⅜˝; cut each diagonally once to make 8 triangles.
		Cut 4 squares 6⅞˝; cut each diagonally once to make 8 triangles.
	Border 1	Cut 4 border strips 2˝ × 34˝.
¼ yard contrasting stripe (cranberry), plaid, or bright color	Border 2	Cut 4 border strips 1½˝ × 36˝.
⅝ yard small floral print	Border 3	Cut 4 border strips 4˝ × 42˝ (selvage to selvage)
½ yard floral print	Binding	Cut 2¾˝ strips to total 178˝ (straight grain or bias).
2⅝ yards fabric	Backing	
Batting, 47˝ × 47˝		

Yardage varies depending on the size of the floral motifs and the number of repeats in the design.

Fabric Requirements and Cutting

Refer to Prewashing Guidelines on
page 8 to determine whether you
will wash your fabrics before cutting
and sewing. See Cutting Techniques,
beginning on page 10, for details on
cutting methods as needed.

Quilt Assembly

Be sure to read Construction Techniques,
page 16, before beginning your project.

1. Assemble the star block as shown in
   the assembly diagram, at right. Refer
   to Stars without Set-in Seams, page 21,
   for specific sewing techniques and
   instructions. Press seams open
   or to one side as desired.

2. Refer to Borders with Butted Corners,
   page 31, and sew the border strips to
   the quilt top in sequence. Press seams
   outward. If you prefer to add mitered
   borders, follow instructions in Mitered
   Borders, page 32.

3. Layer and baste the quilt top with
   batting and backing. Quilt as desired
   and bind.

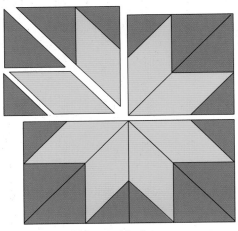

Block assembly diagram

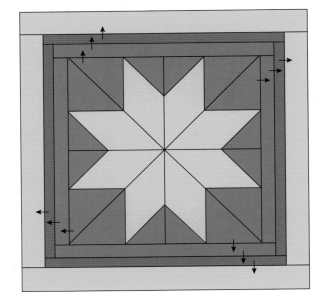

Quilt diagram

Quick LeMoyne Star **with** set-in seams
fast2cut® Fussy Cutter™ 45° diamond ruler, 6½˝
or 6½˝ diamond template pattern, pages 107 and 108
Skill level: Intermediate
Block size: 29˝ × 29˝

IRIS POND

41˝ × 41˝, 2004 by Jan Krentz; quilting by Janet Sturdevant Stuart, Fort Worth, TX

This quilt features a LeMoyne Star with 2 sets of 4 identical diamonds that have been fussy cut from a large-scale iris print. This quilt is perfect for showcasing those lovely floral fabrics that always seem to find their way into our fabric stash. In this quilt, accent trim was sewn to the edges of all 8 diamonds.

Fabric Requirements and Cutting

Refer to Prewashing Guidelines on page 8 to determine whether you will wash your fabrics before cutting and sewing. See Cutting Techniques, beginning on page 10, for details on cutting methods as needed.

Quilt Assembly

Be sure to read Construction Techniques, page 16, before beginning your project.

1. Sew the bright orange-fuchsia accent strips to 2 adjacent edges of the 8 diamonds. Follow the instructions in Sizzling Embellishment: Adding a Sliver of Color on page 28. Trim the excess fabric from the points.

2. Arrange the diamonds and background pieces on a design wall. Assemble the LeMoyne Star as instructed in Stars with Set-In Seams, page 24. Backstitch at the red dots shown in the block assembly diagram below. Press seams between diamonds open; press other seams toward the set-in triangles and squares.

YARDAGE	FOR	CUTTING
1 to 2 yards floral print*	Diamonds	Fussy cut 2 sets of 4 identical diamonds, 6½".
1½ yards purple print	Background	Cut 4 squares 9".
		Cut 1 square 13¼"; cut diagonally twice to yield 4 triangles.
	Border 2	Cut 4 border strips 2½" × 40".
¼ yard bright stripe	Border 1	Cut 4 border strips 1½" × 35".
1⅜ yards dark purple print	Border 3	Cut 4 border strips 3½" × 45" (lengthwise).
	Binding	Cut 2¾" strips to total 176" (straight grain or bias cut).
¼ yard bright orange-fuchsia	Narrow accent trim	Cut 16 strips 1" × 12".
2⅝ yards fabric	Backing	
Batting, 47" × 47"		

Yardage varies depending on size of floral motifs and number of repeats in the design.

3. Sew the 3 border strips together to make a unit, and add them to the quilt following the instructions in Mitered Borders, page 32. Press.

4. Layer and baste the quilt top with batting and backing. Quilt as desired and bind.

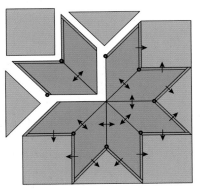

Block assembly diagram; red dots indicate set-in seams.

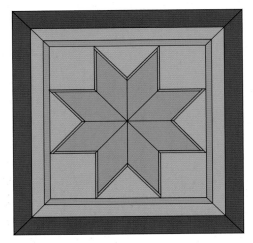

Quilt diagram

Split LeMoyne Star **with** set-in seams
fast2cut® Fussy Cutter™ 45° diamond ruler, 6½˝
or 6½˝ diamond template pattern, pages 107 and 108
Skill level: Intermediate
Block size: 29˝ × 29˝

SUNFLOWER

36˝ × 36˝, 2007 by Jan Krentz; quilting by D'Andrea Mitchell, San Diego, CA

This LeMoyne Star design features split diamonds of 2 different color batik fabrics. Create split diamonds easily by sewing fabric strips together and cutting the diamonds from the strip set. The corner squares and triangles are set-in so that the delightful large-scale sunflower print can be enjoyed undisturbed without the distraction of extra seams. Here's another opportunity to use those large-scale florals.

Fabric Requirements and Cutting

Refer to Prewashing Guidelines on page 8 to determine whether you will wash your fabrics before cutting and sewing. See Cutting Techniques, beginning on page 10, for details on cutting methods as needed.

Quilt Assembly

Be sure to read Construction Techniques, page 16, before beginning your project.

1. Sew the 4¼˝ red-orange strips and 4¼˝ lime green strips together in pairs. Refer to Diamonds Split Lengthwise, page 15. Cut 8 diamonds from the strip sets.

2. Sew the 1˝ cheddar gold accent strips to the diamonds, following the instructions in Sizzling Embellishment: Adding a Sliver of Color, page 28.

YARDAGE	FOR	CUTTING
1½ to 2½ yards floral print*	Background	Cut 4 squares 9˝.
		Cut 1 square 13¼˝; cut diagonally twice to yield 4 triangles.
	Border 1	Cut 4 strips 2½˝ × 35˝.
¾ yard red-orange batik	Split diamonds	Cut 2 strips 4¼˝ × 42˝ (selvage to selvage).
	Border 2	Cut 4 border strips 2˝ × 42˝ (selvage to selvage).
⅝ yard lime green batik	Split diamonds	Cut 2 strips 4¼˝ × 42˝ (selvage to selvage).
	Narrow accent trim in border	Cut 4 strips 1˝ × 42˝ (selvage to selvage).
¼ yard cheddar gold	Narrow accent trim around star points	Cut 16 strips 1˝ × 12˝.
½ yard fabric	Binding	Cut 2¾˝ strips to total 156˝ (straight or bias cut).
1¼ yards fabric	Backing	
Batting, 42˝ × 42˝		

*Purchase the larger amount if you will be fussy cutting. Yardage varies depending on size of floral motifs and number of repeats in the design.

3. Arrange the diamonds and background pieces on a design wall. Assemble the LeMoyne Star, as instructed in Stars with Set-In Seams, page 24. Press seams between diamonds open; press other seams toward the set-in triangles and squares. Backstitch at the red dots shown in the block assembly diagram below.

4. Sew narrow 1˝ accent strips to each red-orange border strip as you did in Step 2. Press and remove bulk as before.

5. Sew the border strips together to make a unit, and add them to the quilt following the instructions in Mitered Borders, page 32. Press.

6. Layer and baste the quilt top with batting and backing. Quilt as desired and bind.

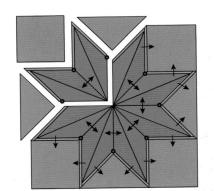

Block assembly diagram; red dots indicate set-in seams.

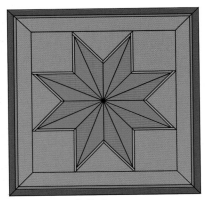

Quilt diagram

Star-in-a-Circle **without** set-in seams

fast2cut® Fussy Cutter™ 45° diamond ruler, 6½˝

or 6½˝ diamond template pattern, pages 107 and 108

Skill level: Intermediate

Star block size: 31½˝ point-to-point

GARDEN VINES

44˝ × 44˝, 2007 by Jan Krentz; quilting by Debra Geissler, Designs by Deb Geissler Enterprises, Inc., Littleton, CO.

This star-in-a-circle may look difficult, but it's really quite easy, so don't be intimidated. It's another chance to have fun with your large-scale fabrics and amaze your friends and family. I used the same fabric for this star as I did for Autumn Leaves, but notice how different the stars look when the diamonds are fussy cut in different ways.

Fabric Requirements and Cutting

Refer to Prewashing Guidelines on page 8 to determine whether you will wash your fabrics before cutting and sewing. See Cutting Techniques, beginning on page 10, for details on cutting methods as needed.

YARDAGE	FOR	CUTTING
1 to 2 yards large-scale or focus fabric*	Diamonds	Fussy cut 8 identical diamonds, 6½″.
1 yard peach	Center star background	Cut 8 and 8r semicircular background wedges (template pattern F, page 110).
1¼ yards dark green print	Background	Cut 1 square 36″.
¼ yard red stripe	Border 1	Cut 4 border strips 1½″ × 42″ (selvage to selvage).
1½ yards floral print	Border 2	Cut 4 border strips 4″ × 48″ (lengthwise).
	Binding	Cut 2¾″ strips to total 188″ (straight grain or bias).
2¾ yards fabric	Backing	
Batting, 50″ × 50″		

Yardage varies depending on size of motifs and number of repeats in the design.

Quilt Assembly

Be sure to read Construction Techniques, page 16, before beginning your project.

1. Arrange the star on a table or design wall with all components in the correct position. Stack all diamonds together, maintaining the same orientation of the print. Stack 8 and 8r background wedges on either side of the diamonds.

2. Construct the star, and appliqué it to the background square as described in Stars in Circles, page 24. Refer to the block assembly diagram, below, for pressing directions.

3. Trim and square up the background to 35½″ × 35½″.

4. Sew the border 1 and 2 strips together as a unit, referring to Mitered Borders, page 32. Add borders to the quilt; press.

5. Layer and baste the quilt top with batting and backing. Quilt as desired and bind.

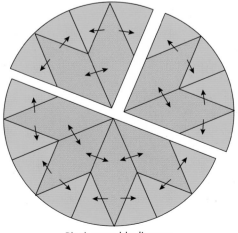

Block assembly diagram

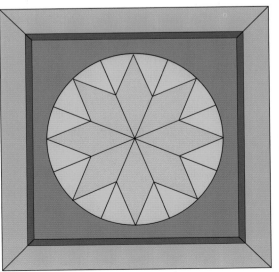

Quilt diagram

Quick Split Star-in-a-Circle *without* set-in seams
fast2cut® Fussy Cutter™ 45° diamond ruler, 6½˝
or 6½˝ diamond template pattern, pages 107 and 108
Skill level: Intermediate
Star block size: 31½˝ point-to-point

WISTERIA

44˝ × 44˝, 2007 by Jan Krentz; quilting by Janet Sturdevant Stuart, Fort Worth, TX.

It's fun to use different fabrics for the diamonds, and here it's double the fun because the diamonds are cut from a strip set of 2 different fabrics. Splitting the diamonds gives the star a more compass-like appearance.

Fabric Requirements and Cutting

Refer to Prewashing Guidelines on page 8 to determine whether you will wash your fabrics before cutting and sewing. See Cutting Techniques, beginning on page 10, for details on cutting methods as needed.

Quilt Assembly

Be sure to read Construction Techniques, page 16, before beginning your project.

1. Sew the 4¼˝ strips together in pairs to create 2 strip sets. Press seams open.

2. Cut 2 diamonds from each strip set; see Diamonds Split Lengthwise, page 15. Remove the remainder of the stitching, and sew the remaining straight edges of each pair of fabrics. Cut 2 additional diamonds from the fabric combinations for a total of 8 (4 from each color combination).

3. Arrange the star on a table or design wall with all components in the correct position. Stack all the diamonds together, maintaining the same orientation for the 2 sets of split diamonds. Stack 8 and 8r background wedges on either side of the diamonds.

YARDAGE	FOR	CUTTING
¼ yard each of the following: medium lavender print light lavender print medium-dark lavender batik pink and lavender print	Split diamonds	Cut 1 strip 4¼˝ × 42˝ (selvage to selvage) of each (4 total).
1 yard light green	Center star background	Cut 8 and 8r semicircular background wedges (template pattern F, page 110).
¼ yard medium lavender	Border 1	Cut 4 border strips 1½˝ × 42˝ (selvage to selvage).
1¼ yards purple and green floral print	Background	Cut 1 square 36˝.
¼ yard light lavender	Narrow accent trim	Cut 4 strips 1˝ × 42˝ (selvage to selvage).
1½ yards pink and lavender print*	Border 2	Cut 4 border strips 4˝ × 48˝ (lengthwise).
½ yard lavender print	Binding	Cut 2¾˝ strips to total 188˝ (straight or bias cut).
2¾ yards fabric	Backing	
Batting, 50˝ × 50˝		

*If you piece the borders, ¾ yard is enough; cut 5 strips 4˝ × 42˝ (selvage to selvage).

4. Construct the star and appliqué it to the background square as described in Stars in Circles, page 24. Refer to the block assembly diagram, below, for pressing directions.

5. Trim and square up the background to 35½˝ × 35½˝.

6. Refer to Sizzling Embellishment: Adding a Sliver of Color, page 28, and sew the narrow accent strips to the lavender border 1 strips.

7. Sew the border 1 and 2 strips together as a unit, referring to Mitered Borders, page 32. Add borders to the quilt; press.

8. Layer and baste the quilt top with batting and backing. Quilt as desired and bind.

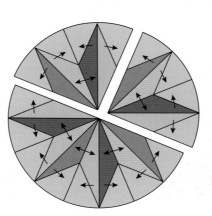

Block assembly diagram

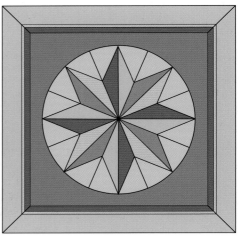

Quilt diagram

Quick Rolling Star **with** set-in seams
fast2cut® Fussy Cutter™ 45° diamond ruler, 6½″
or 6½″ diamond template pattern, pages 107 and 108
Skill level: Intermediate
Block size: 41″ × 41″

PAINTER'S PALETTE

52″ × 52″, 2005 by Jan Krentz; quilting by Janet Sturdevant Stuart, Fort Worth, TX

This easy 32-point star design features diamonds of multiple floral fabrics and a coordinating linear print. Again, this is a perfect quilt for your special floral prints. Who doesn't love sunflowers, geraniums, and ferns! Include your other favorites as well for the look of an old-fashioned cutting garden.

Fabric Requirements and Cutting

Refer to Prewashing Guidelines on page 8 to determine whether you will wash your fabrics before cutting and sewing. See Cutting Techniques, beginning on page 10, for details on cutting methods as needed.

YARDAGE	FOR	CUTTING
1 yard multicolor stripe	Diamonds	Cut 8 diamonds, 6½˝; cut with stripe running lengthwise tip to tip.
2 yards total of assorted floral prints	Diamonds	Cut 24 diamonds, 6½˝.
2¾ yards light floral print*	Border 2	Cut 4 border strips 2½˝ × 68˝; cut parallel to the selvage before cutting other components.
	Background	Cut 16 squares 9⅜˝; cut once diagonally to yield 32 triangles.
		Cut 16 squares 6⅞˝; cut once diagonally to yield 32 triangles.
½ yard yellow print	Border 1	Cut 7 border strips 1½˝ × 42˝ (selvage to selvage).
⅜ yard lime green batik or print	Narrow accent trim	Cut 7 strips 1˝ × 42˝ (selvage to selvage).
⅝ yard fabric	Binding	Cut 2¾˝ strips to total 268˝ (straight grain or bias).
4 yards fabric	Backing	
Batting, 70˝ × 70˝		

*If you want the binding to be the same fabric as the background, you'll need 3⅜ yards.

Quilt Assembly

Be sure to read Construction Techniques, page 16, before beginning your project.

1. Assemble the Snow Crystals block, referring to Stars without Set-In Seams, page 21, and the block assembly diagram, at right. Press the seams as indicated in the diagram.

2. Trim the selvage ends from all 7 of the yellow print 1½˝ strips. Sew the strips together to make 1 long strip. Cut it into 4 pieces, 65˝ long. Repeat with the lime green 1˝ accent strips.

3. Sew a narrow accent strip to the edge of each yellow print border 1 strip as described in Sizzling Embellishment: Adding a Sliver of Color, page 28.

4. Referring to Mitered Borders, page 32, sew borders 1 and 2 together to make border units. Sew the borders to the quilt. Trim and press.

5. Layer and baste the quilt top with batting and backing. Quilt as desired and bind.

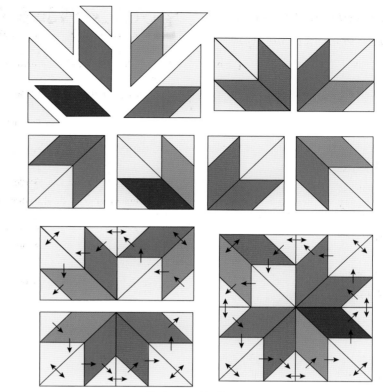

Block assembly diagram

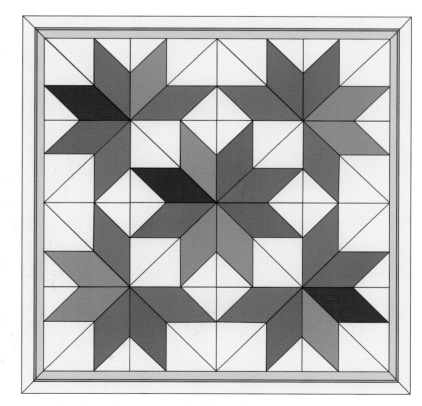

Quilt diagram

Quick Split Snow Crystals *with* set-in seams
fast2cut® Fussy Cutter™ 45° diamond ruler, 6½˝
or 6½˝ diamond template pattern, pages 107 and 108
Skill level: Intermediate/difficult
Block size: 58˝ × 58˝

RAINBOW I

66˝ × 66˝, 2007 by Jan Krentz; quilting by Janet Sturdevant Stuart, Fort Worth, TX

This Snow Crystals quilt features split diamonds in a collection of 16 different fabrics—a medium and darker value fabric for each of the diamonds. Create easy split diamonds by sewing fabric strips together and cutting the diamonds from the strip set. The crisp white background fabric showcases beautiful machine quilting using a pastel variegated thread. The components for the Snow Crystals block are identical to those for the Broken Star design.

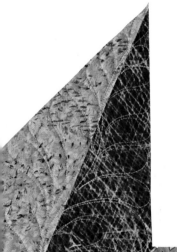

Fabric Requirements and Cutting

Refer to Prewashing Guidelines on page 8 to determine whether you will wash your fabrics before cutting and sewing. See Cutting Techniques, beginning on page 10, for details on cutting methods as needed.

YARDAGE	FOR	CUTTING
2½ yards white	Background	Cut 20 squares 9″.
		Cut 2 squares 13¼″; cut twice diagonally to yield 8 triangles.
	Border 1	Cut 7 border strips 2″ × 42″ (selvage to selvage).
¼ yard each of the following: medium yellow print (1)* darker yellow-orange print (2) medium green print (3) darker green print (4) medium aqua print (5) darker aqua print (6) medium blue print (7) darker blue print (8) medium purple print (9) darker purple print (10) medium orchid purple (11) darker red-violet print (12) medium fuchsia pink (13) darker fuchsia pink (14) medium red print (15) darker red print (16)	Split diamonds	Cut 1 strip 4¼″ × 42″ (selvage to selvage) from each fabric.
⅞ yard multicolor stripe	Border 2	Cut 8 border strips 3″ × 42″ (selvage to selvage, perpendicular to the stripe).
⅝ yard dark print	Binding	Cut 2¾″ strips to total 276″ (straight grain or bias).
4¼ yards fabric	Backing	
Batting, 74″ × 74″		

Numbers in parentheses refer to fabric placement in the quilt diagram, page 70.

Quilt Assembly

Be sure to read Construction Techniques, page 16, before beginning your project.

1. Sew the 4¼″ strips together in pairs to create 8 strip sets, each with a medium and darker value of the same color. Press seams **open**.

2. Cut 2 diamonds from each strip set; see Diamonds Split Lengthwise, page 15. Remove the remainder of the stitching, and sew the remaining straight edges of each pair of fabrics. Cut 2 additional diamonds from the fabric combinations for a total of 32 (4 of each color combination).

3. Sew the Snow Crystals block, referring to the assembly diagram, page 70. See Stars with Set-In Seams, page 24, for specific sewing directions. Press open between diamonds and between squares. Press the other seams toward the squares and triangles.

4. Sew the 7 white border strips together end to end. Cut into 4 strips, 65″ long. Sew the multicolor stripe strips into pairs, and cut to make 4 strips 72″ long.

5. Refer to Mitered Borders on page 32, and sew the borders together into units. Sew borders to the quilt top. Press.

6. Layer and baste the quilt top with batting and backing. Quilt as desired and bind.

Block assembly diagram; red dots indicate set-in seams.

Quilt diagram

Quick and Easy Broken Star *without* set-in seams
fast2cut® Fussy Cutter™ 45° diamond ruler, 6½˝
or 6½˝ diamond template pattern, pages 107 and 108
Skill level: Easy
Block size: 58˝ × 58˝

FRECKLED LILY

70˝ × 70˝, 2007 by Jan Krentz with Lynne Lichtenstern, San Diego, CA; quilting by Debra Geissler, Designs by Deb Geissler Enterprises, Inc., Littleton, CO

This dynamite Broken Star design features fussy-cut diamonds of 2 different fabrics—one floral, one stripe. Fussy cutting requires more yardage to cut identical diamonds from the printed fabric. The surrounding pink background is cut into large and small triangles, so there are no set-in seams, making construction a breeze! Take your time, sew with consistent seam allowances, press as you go, and you'll love the results!

Fabric Requirements and Cutting

Refer to Prewashing Guidelines on page 8 to determine whether you will wash your fabrics before cutting and sewing. See Cutting Techniques, beginning on page 10, for details on cutting methods as needed. Fussy cut all 32 diamonds (see Fussy Cutting Motifs, page 12, and Cutting Diamonds from Stripes, page 13).

YARDAGE	FOR	CUTTING
2 to 3 yards floral print*	Diamonds	Fussy cut 16 diamonds, 6½″.
3½ to 4 yards red-orange-yellow bold stripe	Diamonds	Fussy cut 16 diamonds, 6½″ (feature the same stripe running lengthwise tip to tip in all diamonds).
	Border 2	Cut 8 border strips 4½″ × 42″ (selvage to selvage perpendicular to the stripe).
2½ yards light pink polka dot	Border 1	Cut 4 border strips 2½″ × 66″ (lengthwise).
	Background	Cut 16 squares 9⅜″; cut once diagonally to yield 32 triangles.
		Cut 16 squares 6⅞″; cut once diagonally to yield 32 triangles.
¾ yard fabric	Binding	Cut 2¾″ strips to total 292″ (bias or straight grain).
4¼ yards fabric	Backing	
Batting, 76″ × 76″		

Yardage varies depending on size of floral motifs and number of repeats in design.

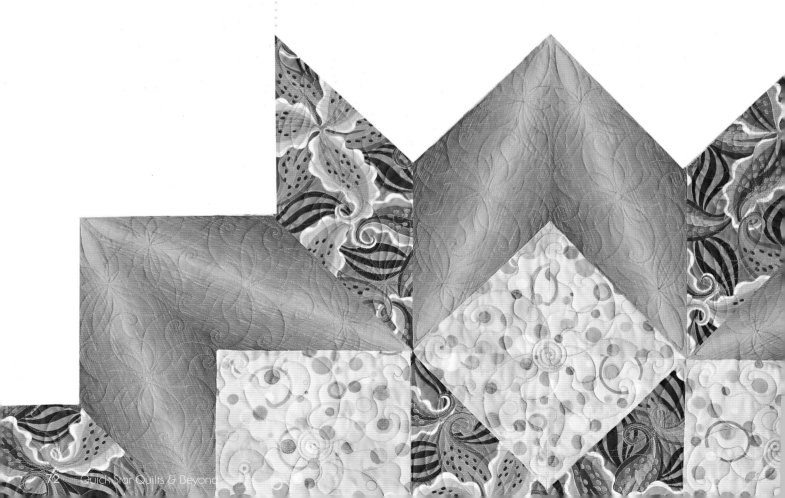

Quilt Assembly

Be sure to read Construction Techniques, page 16, before beginning your project.

1. Sew the Broken Star block, referring to the assembly diagram, at right. See Stars without Set-In Seams, page 21, for specific sewing directions. Follow the arrows in the diagram for pressing directions.

2. Piece the 8 stripe border strips together in pairs and trim to 75″ long.

3. Sew border 1 and border 2 strips together in units as described in Mitered Borders, page 32. Sew borders to the quilt. Press.

4. Layer and baste the quilt top with batting and backing. Quilt as desired and bind.

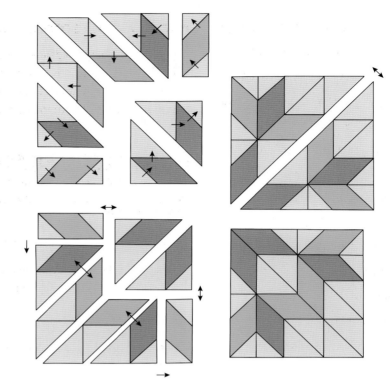

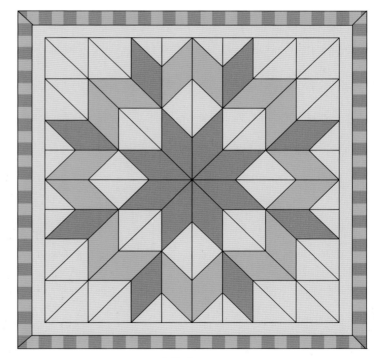

Block assembly diagram

Quilt diagram

Quick Broken Star *with* set-in seams
fast2cut® Fussy Cutter™ 45° diamond ruler, 6½˝
or 6½˝ diamond template pattern, pages 107 and 108
Skill level: Intermediate/difficult
Block size: 58˝ × 58˝

TROPICAL FLING

58˝ × 58˝, 2005 by Jan Krentz; quilting by Janet Sturdevant Stuart, Fort Worth, TX

Parrots in the jungle foliage add the perfect complement to the floral print used in the star diamonds. To keep the parrots as complete as possible, the setting squares and triangles were added with set-in seams. With practice, they're not hard. Choose your own pair of stunning fabrics, add an accent fabric, and you're ready to rock.

Fabric Requirements and Cutting

Refer to Prewashing Guidelines on page 8 to determine whether you will wash your fabrics before cutting and sewing. See Cutting Techniques, beginning on page 10, and Fussy Cutting Motifs, page 12, for details as needed.

YARDAGE	FOR	CUTTING
2 to 3 yards floral with light background*	Diamonds	Fussy cut 32 diamonds, 6½" (The 8 center diamonds are identical; the outer diamonds are cut from various areas in the print.)
2 to 3 yards green tropical print**	Background	Cut 20 squares 9".
		Cut 2 squares 13¼"; cut twice diagonally to yield 8 triangles.
⅛ yard pink and orange tissue lamé	Accent trim (optional)	Cut 16 strips 1" × 12".
⅝ yard fabric	Binding	Cut 2¾" strips to total 244" (bias or straight grain).
3⅝ yards fabric	Backing	
Batting, 64" × 64"		

*Yardage varies depending on size of floral motifs and number of repeats in the design.
**If you do not fussy cut the fabric, 2 yards is enough.

Quilt Assembly

Be sure to read Construction Techniques, page 16, before beginning your project.

1. Sew the narrow trim pieces to the 8 diamonds that will make up the center portion of the star; refer to Sizzling Embellishment: Adding a Sliver of Color, page 28.

2. Sew the Broken Star block, following the assembly diagram, at right. Refer to Stars with Set-In Seams, page 24. Press the seams between diamonds open; press other seams toward the triangles and squares as shown in the quilt diagram, below.

3. Layer and baste the quilt top with batting and backing. Quilt as desired and bind.

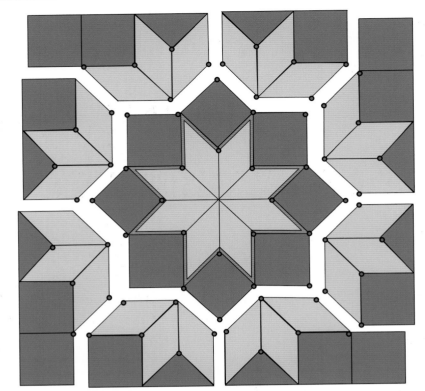

Assembly diagram; red dots indicate set-in seams.

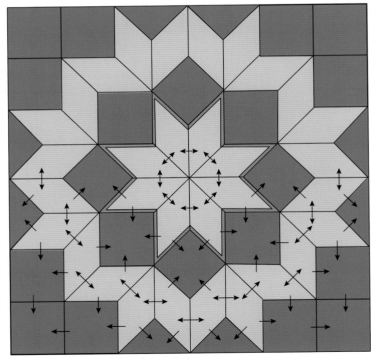

Quilt diagram

Quick Broken Star **with** set-in seams
fast2cut® Fussy Cutter™ 45° diamond ruler, 6½″
or 6½″ diamond template pattern, pages 107 and 108
Skill level: Easy
Block size: 58″ × 58″

RAINBOW II

66″ × 66″, 2007 by Jan Krentz; quilting by Janet Sturdevant Stuart, Fort Worth, TX

This Broken Star design features split diamonds in a collection of 16 different fabrics—a medium and darker value fabric for each diamond. The crisp white background fabric provides a place to highlight fabulous quilting, either by hand or machine. The components for the Broken Star are identical to those for the Snow Crystals design.

Fabric Requirements and Cutting

Refer to Prewashing Guidelines on page 8 to determine whether you will wash your fabrics before cutting and sewing. See Cutting Techniques, beginning on page 10, for details on cutting methods as needed.

YARDAGE	FOR	CUTTING
2½ yards white	Background	Cut 20 squares 9".
		Cut 2 squares, 13¼"; cut diagonally twice to yield 8 triangles.
	Border 1	Cut 7 border strips 2" × 42" (selvage to selvage).
¼ yard each of the following*: medium yellow print (1) darker yellow-orange print (2) medium green print (3) darker green print (4) medium aqua print (5) darker aqua print (6) medium blue print (7) darker blue print (8) medium purple print (9) darker purple print (10) medium orchid purple (11) darker red-violet print (12) medium fuchsia pink (13) darker fuchsia pink (14) medium red print (15) darker red print (16)	Split diamonds	Cut 1 strip 4¼" × 42" (selvage to selvage) of each.
⅞ yard multicolor stripe	Border 2	Cut 8 border strips 3" × 42" (selvage to selvage, perpendicular to the stripe).
⅝ yard fabric	Binding	Cut 2¾" strips to total 276" (straight grain or bias).
4¼ yards fabric	Backing	
Batting, 74" × 74"		

*Numbers in parentheses refer to fabric placement in the quilt diagram, page 29.

Quilt Assembly

Be sure to read Construction Techniques, page 16, before beginning your project.

1. Sew the 4¼″ strips together in pairs to create 8 strip sets, each with a medium and darker value of the same color. Press seams *open*.

2. Cut 2 diamonds from each strip set; see Diamonds Split Lengthwise, page 15. Remove the remainder of the stitching, and sew the remaining straight edges of each pair of fabrics. Cut 2 additional diamonds from the fabric combinations for a total of 32 (4 of each color combination).

3. Sew the Broken Star block, referring to the assembly diagram, at right. See Stars with Set-In Seams, page 24, for specific sewing directions. Press open between diamonds and between squares. Press the other seams toward the squares and triangles.

4. Sew the 7 white border strips together end to end. Cut into 4 strips, 66″ long. Sew the multicolor stripe strips into pairs and cut to make 4 strips 72″ long.

5. Refer to Mitered Borders on page 32, and sew the borders together into units. Sew borders to the quilt top. Press.

6. Layer and baste the quilt top with batting and backing. Quilt as desired and bind.

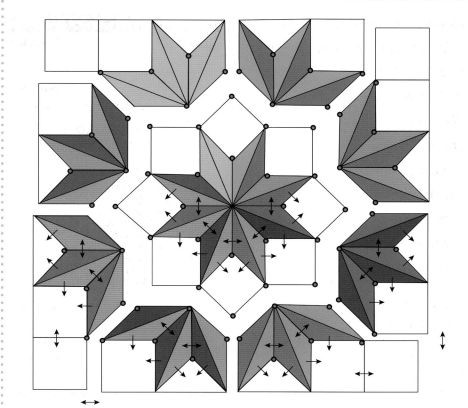

Assembly diagram; red dots indicate set-in seams.

Quilt diagram

Open Star with square center, *with* set-in seams for the center square only
fast2cut® Fussy Cutter™ 45° diamond ruler, 6½″
or 6½″ diamond template pattern, pages 107 and 108
Skill level: Intermediate/difficult
Block size: 46″ × 46″; center square measures 17″ × 17″.

MYTHICAL HORSES

58″ × 58″, 2007 by Jan Krentz; quilting by Debra Geissler, Designs by Deb Geissler Enterprises, Inc., Littleton, CO

This Open Star design features a central square framed by 16 diamonds. A slender dark strip of trim at the edge of the square frames the panel. The border stripe was printed as a companion to the central panel. If your fabric does not have a companion border print, choose a fabric for the border that matches your quilt theme. You can also add multiple borders of different widths, if desired, to create a similar look.

Fabric Requirements and Cutting

Refer to Prewashing Guidelines on page 8 to determine whether you will wash your fabrics before cutting and sewing. See Cutting Techniques, beginning on page 10, for details on cutting methods as needed.

YARDAGE	FOR	CUTTING
⅝ yard focus fabric with large-scale or beautiful design	Center square	Fussy cut 1 square 17½″ (feature your favorite section of the print).
1½ yards blue-green batik	Background	Cut 12 squares 9⅜″; cut once diagonally to yield 24 triangles.
		Cut 4 squares 6⅞″; cut once diagonally to yield 8 triangles.
1¼ to 2 yards fuchsia stripe*	Diamonds	Fussy cut 8 diamonds, 6½″ (cut with stripe running lengthwise tip to tip).
1¼ to 2 yards orange and pink stripe*	Diamonds	Fussy cut 8 diamonds, 6½″ (cut with stripe running lengthwise tip to tip).
⅛ yard dark navy	Narrow accent trim	Cut 4 strips 1″ × 18″.
1⅞ yards border print for lengthwise cut OR 1⅜ yards coordinating fabric for crosswise cut	Border	Cut 4 border strips 6½″ × 66″ OR 7 strips 6½″ × 42″ selvage to selvage.
⅝ yard matching or contrasting fabric	Binding	Cut 2¾″ strips to total 244″ (straight grain or bias).
3⅝ yards	Backing	
Batting, 64″ × 64″		

*Yardage varies depending on the width and repeat of the stripe in the fabric.

Quilt Assembly

Be sure to read Construction Techniques, page 16, before beginning your project.

1. Sew the 1″ narrow contrasting trim strips to the outer edges of the center square as described in Sizzling Embellishment: Adding a Sliver of Color, page 28.

2. Sew the Open Star block, referring to the assembly diagram, at right. You will assemble the 4 sides first as quarter units. Follow the arrows in the diagram for pressing directions.

3. Sew each quarter to a side of the central medallion. Sew the diagonal corner seams, setting-in the center square. Refer to Stars with Set-In Seams, page 24, for details.

4. Refer to Mitered Borders, page 32, to sew the border strips to the quilt. Press.

5. Layer and baste the quilt top with batting and backing. Quilt as desired and bind.

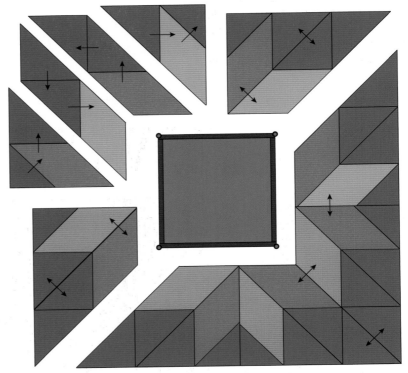

Block assembly diagram; red dots indicate set-in seams.

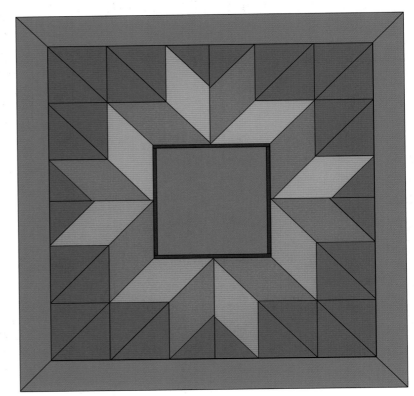

Quilt diagram

Split LeMoyne Open Star, *with* set-in seams
fast2cut® Fussy Cutter™ 45° diamond ruler, 6½˝
or 6½˝ diamond template pattern, pages 107 and 108
Skill level: Intermediate/challenging
Block size: 41˝ × 41˝; center square measures 17˝ × 17˝.

BEWITCHED

45˝ × 45˝, 2007 by Jan Krentz; quilting by Janet Sturdevant Stuart, Fort Worth, TX; binding by Amy Wazny, San Diego, CA

This Open Star design features split diamonds made of three different fabrics. Create easy split diamonds by sewing fabric strips together and cutting the diamonds from the strip set. Fussy cut large prints strategically showcase the motifs within the setting squares and triangles.

Fabric Requirements and Cutting

Refer to Prewashing Guidelines on page 8 to determine whether you will wash your fabrics before cutting and sewing. See Cutting Techniques, beginning on page 10, for details on cutting methods as needed.

YARDAGE	FOR	CUTTING
2 to 3 yards focus fabric*	Center square	Fussy cut 1 square 17½˝.
	Setting squares	Fussy cut 4 squares 9˝ on point.
	Corner triangles	Cut 2 squares 13¼˝; cut twice diagonally to yield 8 triangles. (Or see the tip below to fussy cut the triangles.)
⅝ yard solid black	Split diamonds	Cut 4 strips 4¼˝ × 42˝ (selvage to selvage).
⅜ yard dark fuchsia	Split diamonds	Cut 2 strips 4¼˝ × 42˝ (selvage to selvage).
⅞ yard red-orange stripe	Split diamonds	Cut 2 strips 4¼˝ × 42˝ (selvage to selvage).
	Outer border	Cut 5 border strips 2½˝ × 42˝ (selvage to selvage).
½ yard matching or contrasting color fabric	Binding	Cut 2¾˝ strips to total 192˝ (straight grain or bias).
3 yards fabric	Backing	
Batting, 51˝ × 51˝		

Yardage varies depending on size of motifs and number of repeats in design.

Fussy Cutting Corner Triangles

To fussy cut the corner triangles as I did in my quilt, make a clear template for a quarter-square triangle. For each corner, you need to cut 2 quarter-square triangles and sew them together.

The long side should measure 13¼˝, and the height should be 6⅝˝. See Fussy Cutting Motifs, page 12, for additional details. Mark around the template, and cut out along the marked lines. These measurements include a seam allowance. Try to cut so that the long side is on the straight grain. Otherwise, be very careful when assembling the block, as the outer edges will be bias.

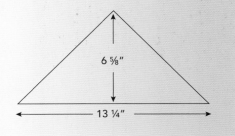

6 ⅝˝

13 ¼˝

Quilt Assembly

Be sure to read Construction Techniques, page 16, before beginning your project.

1. Sew the 4¼˝ black and dark fuchsia strips together in pairs to make 2 strip sets; press the seams open. Refer to Diamonds Split Lengthwise, page 15. Cut 8 diamonds. Repeat with the black and red-orange 4¼˝ strips. Cut 8 diamonds.

2. Sew the block together following the assembly diagram at right. Press in the direction of the arrows.

3. Sew the 2½˝ border strips together to make 1 long strip. Cut into 4 strips, 46˝ long.

4. Refer to Mitered Borders, page 32, and sew the border strips to the quilt. Press.

5. Layer and baste the quilt top with batting and backing. Quilt as desired and bind.

Block assembly diagram; red dots indicate set-in seams.

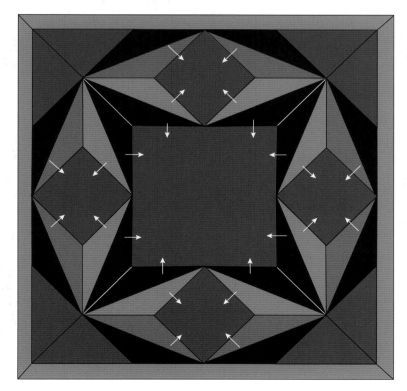

Quilt diagram

LeMoyne Open Star variation, square-on-point setting, *with* set-in seams

fast2cut® Fussy Cutter™ 45° diamond ruler, 6½˝
or 6½˝ diamond template pattern, pages 107 and 108

Skill level: Intermediate/difficult

Block size: 41˝ × 41˝; center square measures 17˝ × 17˝.

GEISHA GARDEN

57˝ × 57˝, 2007 by Jan Krentz; quilting by Janet Sturdevant Stuart, Fort Worth, TX

The handsome Open Star design is perfect to showcase this wonderful geisha fabric. Use the same design to feature **your** favorite fabrics! Select the central focus fabric first; then select the companion fabrics for the surrounding diamonds. Fussy cut larger prints where appropriate, or cut overall printed designs according to the yardage available. You'll be delighted with your masterpiece!

Fabric Requirements and Cutting

Refer to Prewashing Guidelines on page 8 to determine whether you will wash your fabrics before cutting and sewing. See Cutting Techniques, beginning on page 10, for details on cutting methods as needed. Fussy cut the center square from the focus fabric first. Then fussy cut 16 diamonds, all of the same motif, or cut several different print motifs as I did. I cut 4 each of 4 floral motifs and used 1 of each on each side of the center square. See Fussy Cutting Motifs, page 12.

YARDAGE	FOR	CUTTING
2½ to 4 yards* focus fabric	Center square	Cut 1 square 17½″ on point.
	Diamonds	Fussy cut 16 diamonds, 6½″.
1¼ yards lavender or contrasting fabric	Background	Cut 4 squares 9″.
		Cut 2 squares 13¼″; cut diagonally twice to yield 8 triangles .
	Border 1	Cut 5 border strips 2″ × 42″ (selvage to selvage).
⅝ yard black print	Border 2	Cut 5 border strips 2½″ × 42″ (selvage to selvage).
1⅞ yards large colorful floral print	Border 3	Cut 4 border strips 5″ × 62″ (lengthwise).
⅛ yard (optional)**	Narrow accent trim	Cut 4 strips 1″ × 19″.
⅝ yard (optional)***	Binding	Cut 2¾″ strips to total 252″ (straight grain or bias.
3⅝ yards fabric	Backing	
Batting, 63″x 63″		

*Yardage varies depending on size of floral motifs and number of repeats in design
**I did not use a trim in the quilt shown; it depends on your fabric. Apply to outer edges of the center square (not pictured on this quilt)
***If you want the binding to be the same as border 3, you do not need additional binding fabric. Cut the binding strips from the remainder of the floral print.

Quilt Assembly

Be sure to read Construction Techniques, page 16, before beginning your project.

1. Lay out all the quilt components. View from a distance. If desired, audition a slender bit of contrasting color surrounding the center square. Evaluate whether you prefer the design with or without the accent strip. If you want the accent strips, sew the 4 narrow trim strips to the center square now. See Sizzling Embellishment: Adding a Sliver of Color, page 28, for details. Press.

2. Sew the block together, assembling the diamonds into units first, and setting in the seams for the squares and side triangles as shown in the assembly diagram, at right. Press the seams open between the diamonds and toward the squares and triangles. Sew the diamond units to each side of the center square, and sew the diagonal seams, referring to Stars with Set-In Seams, page 24. Press as shown in the diagram.

3. Sew border 1 strips together end to end to make a long strip; cut it into 4 equal lengths. Repeat with the border 2 strips.

4. Referring to Mitered Borders, page 32, sew all of the border strips together into units and sew them to the quilt. Press.

5. Layer and baste the quilt top with batting and backing. Quilt as desired and bind.

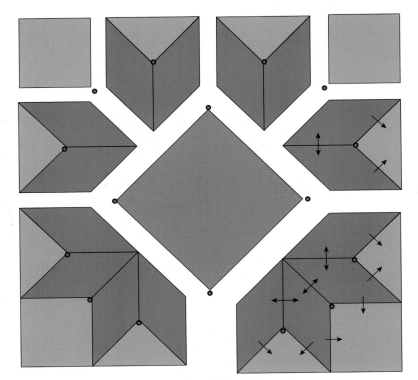

Block assembly diagram; red dots indicate set-in seams.

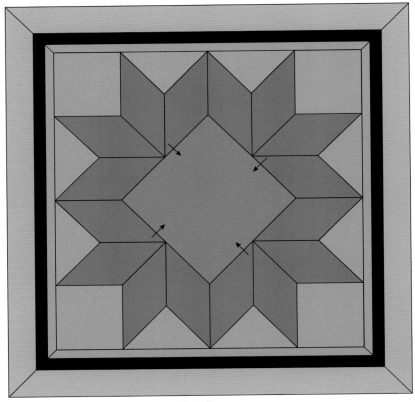

Quilt diagram

Quick Starburst or Sunburst **without** set-in seams
fast2cut® Fussy Cutter™ 45° diamond ruler, 6½˝ or 3˝
or 6½˝ diamond template pattern, pages 107 and 108
or 3˝ diamond template pattern, page 107
Skill level: Easy

COLOR STRIPES

110˝ × 110˝, 2007 by Jan Krentz with R. Lynne Lichtenstern, San Diego, CA;
quilting by Debra Geissler, Designs by Deb Geissler Enterprises, Inc., Littleton, CO

This traditional Starburst or Sunburst design is a modern version of a one-patch quilt design. Cut a variety of fabrics into 3″ or 6½″ diamonds and arrange them on a design wall. The larger diamonds will create a large quilt very quickly! The biggest challenge will be deciding when the quilt is done and you are ready to trim the edges.

Fabric choices will greatly influence the appearance of your quilt. Include some fussy-cut units intermingled with batik fabrics, or create string-pieced strip sets and cut them into diamonds.

Fabric Requirements and Cutting

Refer to Prewashing Guidelines on page 8 to determine whether you will wash your fabrics before cutting and sewing. See Cutting Techniques, beginning on page 10, for details on cutting methods as needed.

Use the chart below and the diagrams, page 91, to decide what size quilt you wish to make: small, medium, or large. This quilt can be made using either size Fussy Cutter™ ruler. Collect fabrics from your stash and cut diamonds in multiples of 8 to create a symmetrical design. Eight diamonds create the center star, and each successive round will have 8 additional diamonds (16, 24, 32, etc.). If you prefer an asymmetrical color placement in your quilt, you might want to photocopy the diagram on page 91 and color in the diamonds to estimate the numbers to cut of various fabrics. The yardage estimates are a guideline only. This is a good quilt to use fabrics from your stash.

Before cutting, press your fabrics; then cut up to 4 layers at once using a sharp new 45mm or 60mm rotary cutter. Save any partial fabric pieces remaining at the edges; you may be able to use them at the edges of the quilt top.

QUILT SIZE*	YARDAGE	NUMBER OF DIAMONDS TO CUT	DIAMOND RULER SIZE
25″ × 25″ (Outline A)	1 to 3+ yards total	84–100	3″
60″ × 60″ (Outline A)	5 to 8+ yards total	84–100	6½″
35″ × 35″ (Outline B)	2 to 4+ yards total	160–200	3″
84″ × 84″ (Outline B)	9 to 13+ yards total	160–200	6½″
46″ × 46″ (Outline C)	3 to 6+ yards total	276–300	3″
110″ × 110″ (Outline C)	14 to 20+ yards total	276–300	6½″

Small, medium, or large piece of flannel, flannel sheet, flannel-backed tablecloth, or batting for designing the quilt.

Backing and batting: add 6″ to 8″ to the quilt size.

Binding yardages: ⅜ yard, ⅝ yard, ½ yard, ⅞ yard, ½ yard, 1 yard (in chart order)

*See the quilt diagrams, page 91, for outlines of the various sizes.

Quilt Assembly

Be sure to read Construction Techniques, page 16, before beginning your project. A design wall will make it much easier when laying out the diamonds for this quilt.

1. Determine whether your quilt design will be centered (as in the quilt shown), or if the star will be off-center. Using your flannel, press folds as described below to create a guide for arranging the diamonds. As an alternative, you might mark your existing design wall with tape to create a guide.

- **For a symmetrical, centered design:** Fold the flannel in half lengthwise and crosswise. Press the folds to make prominent creases. Fold the flannel diagonally in both directions and press the folds. The flannel will be divided equally into 8 sections with all folds intersecting in the middle.

- **For an off-center or asymmetrical design:** Evenly fold a section (approximately ⅓) of the flannel lengthwise, creating a strip parallel to the edge. Press the fold. Rotate the flannel, and fold a strip (approximately ⅓) of the flannel widthwise. Press the fold. Fold the flannel diagonally, matching the first creases. Press the diagonal creases.

2. Mount the flannel on a wall, a large piece of cardboard, or a large sheet of foam insulation board.

3. Arrange the diamonds, beginning in the center. Align diamonds in the sections, using the creases to keep the 8 sections orderly. Fill in the edges of the diamond rows with the scraps left over during the cutting process.

4. Assemble the diagonal rows of diamonds, pressing seams open. Use spray starch to stabilize the rows and prevent stretching or distortion.

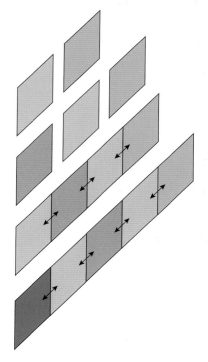

5. Assemble the rows, creating 8 sections. Sew pairs of sections, creating 4 quarter sections. Press the seam open between units.

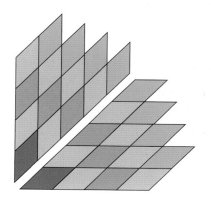

6. Assemble the quarter units into halves; finally join the 2 halves, aligning the center intersection. Pin the intersections along the entire length of the seam and sew the quilt top. The outer edges will be very irregular and ragged at this stage.

7. Press the quilt top neatly; lay the quilt top face down on a large cutting mat. Fold the quilt in half and align the longest straight ruler *perpendicular with the fold.* Trim the double layers at both ends that are stacked together. Unfold and repeat by folding in the opposite direction and trimming the remaining 2 edges.

Note: if your trimmed quilt top is smaller than you desire, design and add borders to coordinate with the quilt.

8. Layer and baste the quilt top with batting and backing. Quilt as desired and bind.

Symmetrical quilt diagram in 3 sizes

Asymmetrical quilt diagram in 3 sizes

Touching LeMoyne Star **with** set-in seams
fast2cut® Fussy Cutter™ 45° diamond ruler, 3˝
or 3˝ diamond template pattern, page 107
Skill level: Intermediate
Block size: 12˝ × 12˝

ASIAN FLAIR

46˝ × 58˝, 2007 by Jan Krentz; quilting by Janet Sturdevant Stuart, Fort Worth, TX

This Touching LeMoyne Star quilt is a contemporary version of an old favorite—12 blocks set side-by-side were cut with the 3˝ diamond ruler.

This quilt features a collection of several different red, black, and yellow prints to create a scrap quilt look. Select prints that are similar in character, yet different enough to be interesting when used in the same quilt. Fabric may be purchased as standard eighth-, quarter-, and half-yard cuts, as well as fat eighths (9˝ × 21˝) and fat quarters (18˝ × 21˝).

Fabric Requirements and Cutting

Refer to Prewashing Guidelines on page 8 to determine whether you will wash your fabrics before cutting and sewing. See Cutting Techniques, beginning on page 10, for details on cutting methods as needed. After pressing your fat quarters and fat eighths, layer as many as you are comfortable cutting through to cut strips, diamonds, and squares as instructed.

YARDAGE	FOR	CUTTING
⅛ yard or 1 fat eighth each of 6 yellow prints*	Diamonds	Cut 3˝ strips; subcut 8 diamonds, 3˝, from each fabric (48 total).
⅜ yard yellow print	Border 1	Cut 5 border strips 1½˝ × 42˝ (selvage to selvage).
¼ yard or 1 fat quarter each of 6 red prints	Diamonds	Cut 4 diamonds, 3˝, from each fabric (24 total).
	Background of 6 blocks	Cut 4 squares, 4˝, from each fabric (24 total). Cut 1 square, 6¼˝, from each fabric; cut twice diagonally to yield 4 triangles (24 total).
¼ yard red print	Narrow red accent trim	Cut 5 strips 1˝ × 42˝ (selvage to selvage).
¼ yard or 1 fat quarter each of 6 different black prints*	Diamonds	Cut 4 diamonds, 3˝, from each fabric (24 total).
	Background of 6 blocks	Cut 4 squares, 4˝, from each fabric (24 total). Cut 1 square, 6¼˝, from each fabric; cut twice diagonally to yield 4 triangles (24 total).
1¾ yards black print	Border 2	Cut 2 border strips 4½˝ × 50˝. Cut 2 border strips 4½˝ × 62˝.
	Binding	Cut 2¾˝ strips to total 220˝ (straight grain or bias).
3 yards fabric	Backing	
Batting, 50˝ × 62˝		

*For scrappier blocks, use 12 different prints; cut 4 diamonds from each.

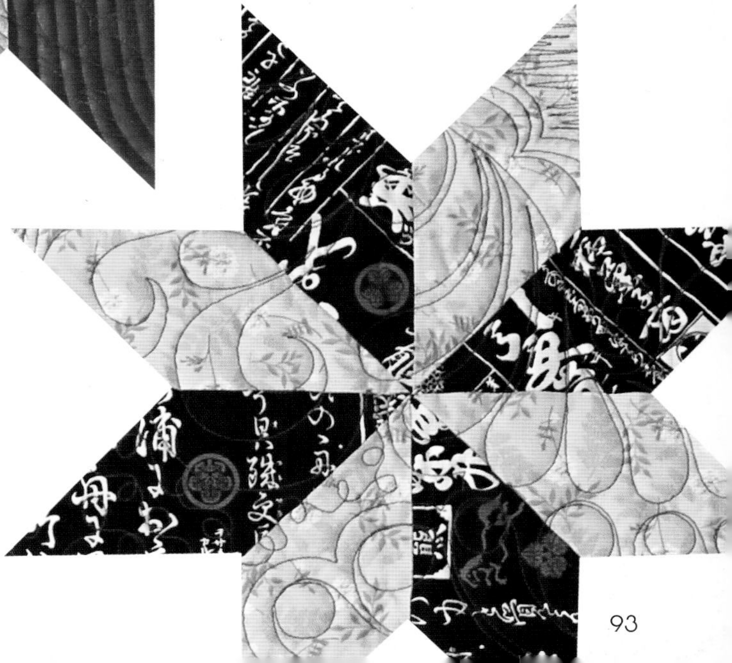

Quilt Assembly

Be sure to read Construction Techniques, page 16, before beginning your project.

1. Arrange the star blocks with all components in the correct position. Each block will contain 4 matching yellow diamonds and 4 matching red or black diamonds. (Note that I mixed 2 of the red and black diamonds in a couple of blocks to make them scrappier.) Use background squares and triangles cut from the same red or black print.

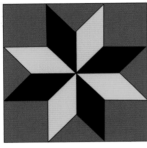

Make 6.

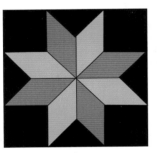

Make 6.

2. Assemble the star blocks with set-in seams; see Stars with Set-In Seams, page 24, for detailed instructions, and refer to the block assembly diagram at right. Press the seams between the diamonds open or to the side as desired. Press the remaining seams toward the triangles and squares.

3. Arrange the blocks into 4 rows of 3 blocks each. Refer to the quilt diagram, below, for placement details. Sew the blocks into rows, pressing seams to the side, in opposite direction from row to row.

4. Sew the rows together, pressing the seams in one direction.

5. Piece the narrow red trim strips together to make 1 long strip. Cut it into 2 strips 50″ long and 2 strips 62″ long. Sew them to the black border strips, according to the directions in Sizzling Embellishment: Adding a Sliver of Color, page 28. Press.

6. Sew yellow and black border strips together with the narrow red trim in between. See Mitered Borders, page 32, and attach the border units to the quilt with the yellow next to the blocks. Press.

7. Layer and baste the quilt top with batting and backing. Quilt as desired and bind.

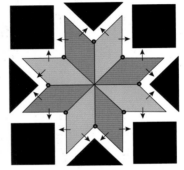

Block assembly diagram;
red dots indicate set-in seams.

Quilt diagram

Quick Touching Stars/Open Star variation **with** set-in seams
fast2cut® Fussy Cutter™ 45° diamond ruler, 6½˝
or 6½˝ diamond template pattern, pages 107 and 108
Skill level: Intermediate/challenging
Block size: 29˝ × 29˝; large squares measure 17˝ × 17˝.

ROOSTER MAGNIFICO

91˝ × 91˝, 2007 by Jan Krentz with R. Lynne Lichtenstern, San Diego, CA; quilting by Susanne Fagot, El Cajon, CA

Like the rooster, this magnificent quilt will announce its individuality, varying with the fabrics that you choose. Find your focus fabric first, and let that dictate your colors. You can probably find plenty of fabrics for the split diamonds on your own fabric shelves, but don't hesitate to pick up some additional fabrics to coordinate with the focus fabric when you're out shopping.

Fabric Requirements and Cutting

Refer to Prewashing Guidelines on page 8 to determine whether you will wash your fabrics before cutting and sewing. See Cutting Techniques, beginning on page 10, for details on cutting methods as needed.

YARDAGE	FOR	CUTTING
3½ to 4 yards theme print with interesting medium to large motifs	Squares	Fussy cut 4 squares 17½", on point.
	Block corners	Cut 2 squares 9⅜"; cut once diagonally to yield 4 triangles.
	Setting triangles	Cut 2 squares, 25⅜"; cut diagonally twice to yield 8 triangles.
2¾ yards green print	Split diamonds	Cut 1 strip 4¼" × 42" (lengthwise).
	Border 2	Cut 4 border strips 3½" × 96" (lengthwise).
⅞ yard black print	Split diamonds	Cut 1 strip 4¼" × 42" (selvage to selvage).
	Border 1	Cut 9 border strips 2" × 42" (selvage to selvage).
1½ yards total assorted light and medium green prints	Split diamonds	Cut 9 strips 4¼" × 42" (selvage to selvage).
1¾ yards total assorted red prints	Split diamonds	Cut 10 strips 4¼" × 42" (selvage to selvage).
1¼ yards total assorted black prints	Split diamonds	Cut 7 strips 4¼" × 42" (selvage to selvage).
1 yard gold print	Split diamonds	Cut 4 strips 4¼" × 42" (selvage to selvage).
	Block corners	Cut 2 squares 9⅜"; cut once diagonally to yield 4 triangles.
⅜ yard ivory print	Block corners	Cut 2 squares 9⅜"; cut once diagonally to yield 4 triangles.
⅝ yard yellow print	Block corners	Cut 4 squares 9⅜"; cut once diagonally to yield 8 triangles.
⅝ yard medium tan print	Block corners	Cut 6 squares 9⅜"; cut once diagonally to yield 12 triangles.
⅞ yard fabric	Binding	Cut 2¾" strips to total 376" (straight grain or bias).
8½ yards fabric or 2⅞ yards 108"-wide fabric	Backing	
Batting, 99" × 99"		

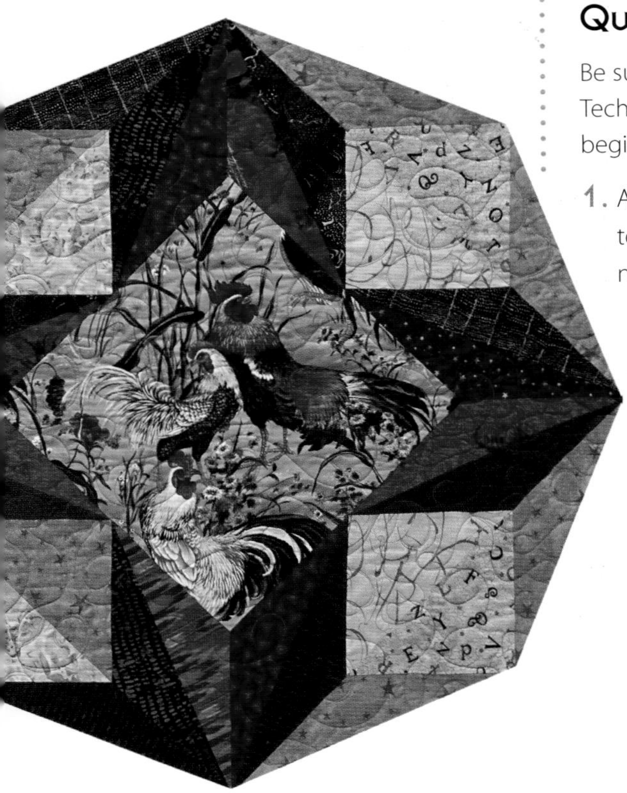

Quilt Assembly

Be sure to read Construction Techniques, page 16, before beginning your project.

1. Arrange and sew the 4¼" strips together in the following combinations; press the seams open.

Make 2.

Make 2.

Make 4.

Make 4.

Make 4.

2. Referring to Diamonds Split Lengthwise, page 15, cut diamonds from the strip combinations. You should have the following number and color of split diamonds for a total of 64.
   - 8 green / gold
   - 8 red-orange / gold
   - 16 red / green
   - 16 green / black
   - 16 red / black

3. Arrange all of the pieces in the correct position on a design wall. Refer to the photograph on page 95 for placement guidance

4. Sew a triangle between pairs of diamonds, following the assembly diagram, at right.

5. Sew 1 diamond-triangle-diamond unit to each edge of the squares and triangles cut from the theme fabric, stopping and backstitching at both ends of the seam. See Stars with Set-In Seams, page 24. Press seams toward the squares and triangles.

6. Sew the diagonal seams, joining diamonds at the corners of each unit. Press seams open. Make 4 square and 8 triangle sections.

7. Join sections together in diagonal rows as shown in the assembly diagram. Press seams open between all sections. Join diagonal sections together into halves. Press. Sew the 2 diagonal halves together across the center. Press.

8. Sew the border 1 strips together. Cut into 4 lengths, 90˝ long.

9. Refer to Mitered Borders, page 32. Sew the border 1 strips to the border 2 strips to make border units. Attach the borders to the quilt top and press.

10. Layer and baste the quilt top with batting and backing. Quilt as desired and bind.

Assembly diagram; red dots indicate set-in seams.

Quilt diagram

Quick Kaleidoscope
fast2cut® half-diamond ruler, 6½˝
or 6½˝ half-diamond template pattern, page 109
Skill level: Easy
Block size: 15½˝ × 15½˝

FLYING COLORS

56½˝ × 56½˝, 2007 by Jan Krentz, Poway, CA with R. Lynne Lichtenstern, San Diego, CA;
quilting by Janet Sturdevant Stuart, Fort Worth, TX; and Jan Krentz

This great quilt features 9 blocks cut with the 6 ½″ half-diamond ruler. Fabric choice will dictate the overall personality of your quilt—the quilt pictured here uses 2 main fabrics, a Laurel Burch hummingbird print and a blue-green batik. Corner triangles in an accent color add interest to the overall design.

Fabric Requirements and Cutting

Refer to Prewashing Guidelines on page 8 to determine whether you will wash your fabrics before cutting and sewing. See Cutting Techniques, beginning on page 10, for details on cutting methods as needed. Note: you can cut 9 half-diamonds from a full-width strip.

YARDAGE	FOR	CUTTING
1¼ yards light whimsical print	Half-diamonds	Cut 4 strips 8¾″ × 42″. Subcut the strips using the 6½″ half-diamond template pattern, page 109 to yield 36 half diamonds.
1¼ yards blue-green batik	Half-diamonds	Cut 4 strips 8¾″ × 42″. Subcut the strips using the 6½″ half-diamond template pattern, page 109 to yield 36 half diamonds.
½ yard blue	Corner triangles	Cut 2 strips 5½″ × 42″. Subcut into 8 squares 5½″; cut once diagonally to yield 16 triangles.
½ yard total of assorted pink/yellow/orange prints	Corner triangles	Cut a total of 10 squares 5½″. Cut once diagonally to yield 20 triangles.
⅞ yard accent color	Border 1	Cut 5 strips 1½″ × 42″.
	Binding	Cut 2¾″ strips to total 238″ (straight grain or bias).
1 yard medium- to large-scale bright floral print	Border 2	Cut 6 strips 4½″ × 42″ (selvage to selvage).
3⅝ yards fabric	Backing	
Batting, 63″ × 63″		

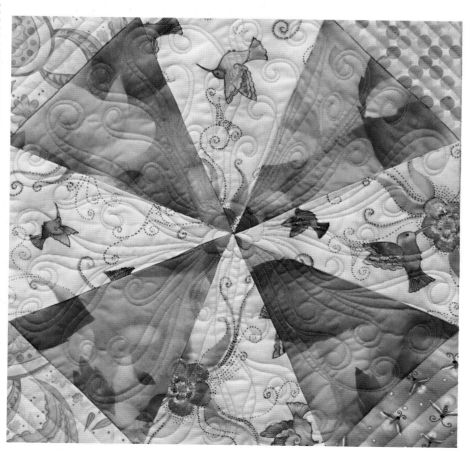

Quilt Assembly

Be sure to read Construction Techniques, page 16, before beginning your project. Refer to Mastering the Eight-Pointed Intersection, Method Two: Seams Pressed Open, page 20, as needed when sewing the blocks.

1. Sew half-diamond pairs with your 2 fabrics. *Always sew with the same fabric on the top of the pair,* sewing all 36 pairs in the same direction, raw edge to raw edge.

2. Trim the tips of the half-diamond pairs as described on page 20. Press the seams open.

3. Sew 2 pairs of half-diamonds together to create 18 units. Press the seams open. Sew these units together to create 9 octagonal blocks.

4. Arrange the blocks referring to the assembly diagram, at right, and the photograph, page 98. Note the orientation of the light and dark pieces changes from one block to the next. Position the corner triangles as shown in the photo.

5. Work with 1 block at a time. Position the 4 corner triangles right sides together on the octagonal unit. Pin to hold them securely. Sew the triangles to the edges of the octagon. Press the seams *open* on all 9 blocks *or* press the seams to the side in alternating directions from block to block so the seams will butt together.

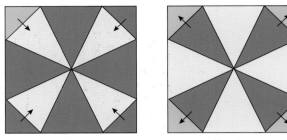

+ pattern   X pattern
Press seams in opposite direction from block to block.

6. Sew the blocks into rows. Press seams open or to the side in opposite direction from row to row.

7. Sew the rows together. Press.

8. Sew border 1 strips end to end, creating 1 long strip. Cut into 4 pieces of equal length.

9. Sew the border 2 strips end to end, creating 1 long strip. Cut into 4 pieces of equal length.

10. Refer to Mitered Borders, page 32, to make border units and sew them to the quilt. Press.

11. Layer and baste the quilt top with batting and backing. Quilt as desired and bind.

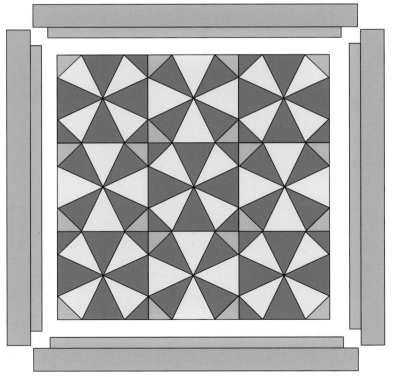

Quilt assembly diagram

Quick Kaleidoscope
fast2cut® half-diamond ruler, 3˝
or 3˝ half-diamond template pattern, page 108
Skill level: Easy
Block size: 6¾˝ × 6¾˝

KALEIDOSCOPE DOWN UNDER

73˝ × 59˝, 2007 by Jan Krentz; quilting by Susanne Fagot, El Cajon, CA; Janet Sturdevant Stuart, Fort Worth, TX; and Jan Krentz

This travel collage quilt features 63 Kaleidoscope blocks using fabrics collected during my 2007 teaching trip to New Zealand and Australia. I was so eager to use the fabrics that I began piecing the small blocks by hand on the airplane. This is a perfect quilt for conversation prints—fabrics with whimsical prints or specific themes. The fabrics in the quilt shown feature imagery from the plants, wildlife, and people of New Zealand and Australia.

Fabric Requirements and Cutting

Refer to Prewashing Guidelines on page 8 to determine whether you will wash your fabrics before cutting and sewing. See Cutting Techniques, beginning on page 10, for details on cutting methods as needed. Cut half-diamonds using the half-diamond ruler, rotary cutter, and a small mat; a rotating cutting mat is helpful for cutting around the half-diamond ruler. Alternatively, use the 3″ half-diamond template pattern, page 108.

Jan's Tip

Alternate boldly patterned fabrics with calmer tone-on-tone fabrics if you want to distinctly see the pieced areas. For blended patterns with less visible geometric piecing, use patterned fabrics in all 8 half-diamond triangles and corner triangles.

YARDAGE	FOR	CUTTING
2¼ yards fabric with color gradation*	Borders	Cut 4 lengthwise strips 6½″ wide or 7 strips crosswise, depending on the colors and how they flow through the fabric.
2 to 3 yards total of interesting fabrics, scraps, and conversation prints in fat eighths and fat quarters	Half-diamonds	Cut a total of 252 half-diamonds using the 3″ half-diamond template pattern, page 108. Cut extra for design flexibility if desired.
2¾ to 3½ yards total of tone-on-tone or solid fabrics in fat eighths and fat quarters**	Half-diamonds	Cut a total of 252 half-diamonds using the 3″ half-diamond template pattern, page 108. Cut extra for design flexibility if desired.
	Corner triangles	Cut a total of 126 squares 2⅞″. Cut once diagonally to yield 252 triangles. Cut extra for design flexibility if desired.
⅝ yard fabric	Binding	Cut 2¾″ strips to total 278″ (straight grain or bias)
3¾ yards fabric	Backing	
Batting, 79″ × 65″		

If you want the binding to be the same fabric as the border, purchase 2¾ yards.
**See Jan's Tip below. You may want to substitute prints for the tone-on-tone or solid fabrics.*

Quilt Assembly

Be sure to read Construction Techniques, page 16, before beginning your project. Refer to Mastering the Eight-Pointed Intersection, Method Two: Seams Pressed Open, page 20, as needed when sewing the blocks.

1. Working on a large flannel design wall, lay out the various fabric triangles, creating blocks in an alternating "+" and "X" pattern (as shown in the blocks on page 100). Create a color-wash effect by grouping areas of light colors together and surrounding the light areas with slightly darker colors, working toward sections with different shades and colors. Lay out the blocks in 7 rows of 9 blocks each.

2. Once you are happy with the arrangement, sew one block together at a time. Work systematically from block to block, sewing the half-diamonds into octagons first. Follow Steps 1 to 4 on page 100 to construct the octagonal sections. Do not sew the corner triangles to the octagons yet. Press the octagons. Return the completed units to the design wall. Take another look at your design, and make any final rearrangements of the blocks and corner triangles.

3. Sew triangles to the corresponding corners of all 63 octagons. Pay attention to the orientation of the darker "+" and "X" pattern within each octagon. This creates the overall circular illusion. Establish the pressing sequence for the triangles; press all "+" blocks toward the octagonal center, and press all "X" blocks toward the triangles. Trim and square up the corners of the blocks as needed. They should measure 7¼″ × 7¼″.

4. Sew the blocks together in rows, pressing the seams in the opposite direction from row to row.

5. Sew the rows together, pressing the seams in one direction as you go.

6. Audition border strips around the quilt top, cutting and sewing seams to create a graduated color flow that enhances, frames, and expands the color flow within the blocks.

7. Refer to Mitered Borders, page 32, to add the borders to the quilt.

8. *Optional:* appliqué theme cutouts or souvenir patches throughout the composition or in the borders.

9. Layer and baste the quilt top with batting and backing. Quilt as desired and bind.

Quilt diagram

Quick Harbor Lights/Signal Lights variation
fast2cut® half-diamond ruler, 6½˝, and fast2cut® Fussy Cutter™ 45° diamond ruler, 3˝
or 6½˝ half-diamond template pattern, page 109 and 3˝ diamond template pattern, page 107
Skill level: Easy
Block size: 15½˝ × 15½˝

SUNSET POINT

62˝ × 62˝, 2007 by Jan Krentz; quilting by Carolyn Reynolds, Acton, CA

This quilt features sixteen blocks based on the traditional **Harbor Lights** or **Signal Lights** block. Create the entire quilt using all the same block design, or create a pseudoborder by simplifying the outer row of blocks, as seen in the photograph. Simply add more blocks to increase the finished quilt size.

Fabric Requirements and Cutting

Refer to Prewashing Guidelines on page 8 to determine whether you will wash your fabrics before cutting and sewing. See Cutting Techniques, beginning on page 10, for details on cutting methods as needed. To cut the appliquéd half-diamond triangles, use the 3″ fast2cut® Fussy Cutter™ 45° diamond guide ruler. Then cut the diamonds in half across the center.

YARDAGE	FOR	CUTTING
3½ to 4 yards total of red prints in fat eighths, fat quarters, and scraps	Half-diamond triangles	Cut a total of 64 large half-diamond triangles using the 6½″ half-diamond template pattern, page 109.
	Half-diamond triangles for appliqués	Cut a total of 18 diamonds 3″ using the 3″ diamond template pattern, page 107; cut in half across the center to create 36 small half-diamond triangles.
	Corner triangles	Cut a total of 32 squares 5½″; cut once diagonally to yield 64 triangles.
2¼ yards total of gold prints in fat quarters, fat eighths, and scraps	Half-diamond triangles	Cut a total of 64 half-diamond triangles using the 6½″ half-diamond template pattern, page 109.
⅝ yard black print	Binding	Cut 2¾″ strips to total 260″ (straight grain or bias cut).
4 yards fabric	Backing	
Batting, 68″ × 68″		

ADDITIONAL TOOLS AND SUPPLIES

Lightweight paper-backed fusible web or precut fusible hem adhesive (sold on rolls); cut into 36 strips ½″ × 10″.

Freezer paper (You can substitute brown craft paper or scrap fabric to protect your ironing surface.)

Appliqué pressing sheet or 18″ to 24″ piece of baking parchment paper

Optional: small-size or rotating rotary-cutting mat to easily cut small shapes from scraps of fabric

Quilt Assembly

Be sure to read Construction Techniques, page 16, before beginning your project.

1. Cover your ironing board surface by ironing a piece of freezer paper, shiny side down, to the cover. Use craft paper or old scrap fabric if you prefer.

2. Lay the small triangles wrong side up on the ironing board in rows, as shown, having the edges touching but not overlapping. Carefully lay a ½″ strip of fusible web (pebbly side down) over the raw edges, centering it over the triangles on either side. Trim the ends of the strips as needed. Cover with an appliqué pressing sheet or baking parchment paper. Press to adhere fusible web to fabrics. Continue until all of the small triangles have approximately ¼″ of fusible web along all raw edges.

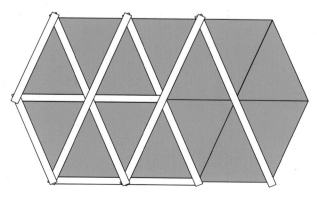

3. Carefully peel the paper backing off the small red triangles, and cut the fusible web between the pieces with scissors. Trim any threads that have raveled at the raw edges.

4. Fold 36 yellow triangles in half, pinching a center crease along the shortest side.

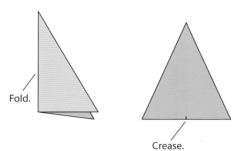

Fold.

Crease.

5. Position the smaller red triangles on the right side of the yellow triangles as shown, aligning the point of the triangle with the crease, ¼″ from the edge. Press to fuse the layers together. The small triangles should **not** extend into the seam allowances of the larger yellow triangles.

Make 36.

6. Machine appliqué the triangles in place by stitching along the raw edges with your favorite stitch. I used a machine blanket stitch.

7. Working on a large flannel design wall, lay out the various fabric triangles, creating the overall pattern according to the assembly diagram, at right, and photo, page 104. In this quilt, the gold triangles form an × in each block. Arrange the blocks in 4 rows of 4 blocks each. Position the pieces without appliqué along the outer edges to create the "border."

8. Remove the units for one block at a time and sew the triangles together, following Steps 1 to 4, page 100, to create the octagon unit. Press the seams open. Then sew the corner triangles to the octagons. Press the seams in alternating directions from one block to the next so that the seams will butt together.

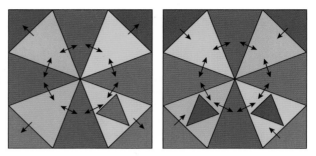

9. Sew the blocks together in rows, pressing the seams in opposite direction from row to row. Sew the rows together, pressing the seams in one direction.

10. Layer and baste the quilt top with batting and backing. Quilt as desired and bind.

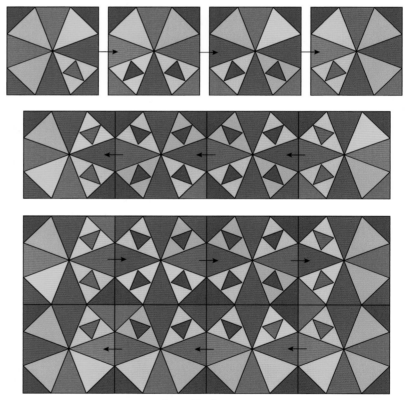

Assembly diagram

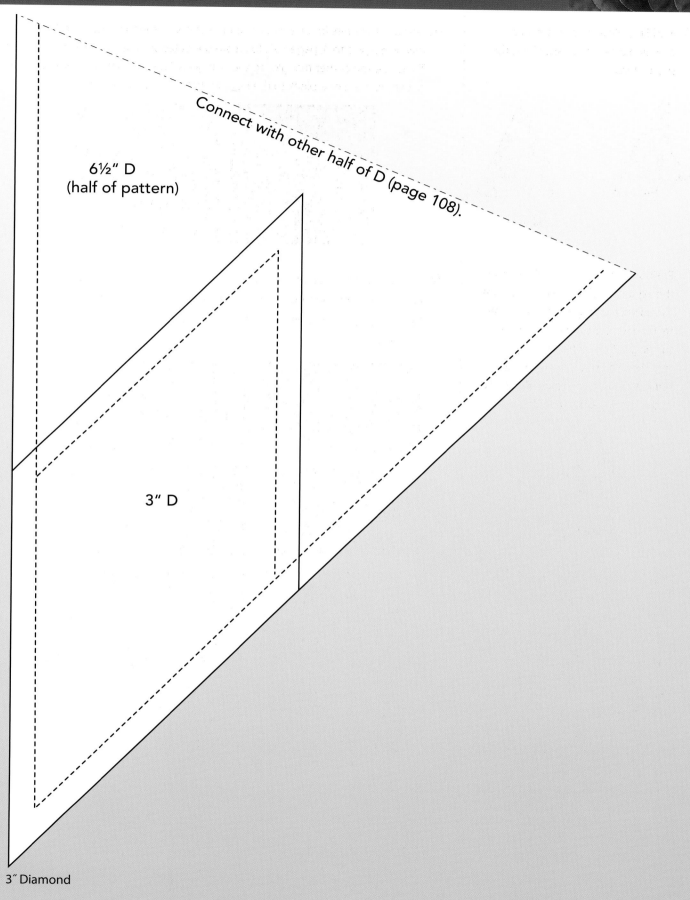

6½" D
(half of pattern)

Connect with other half of D (page 108).

3" D

3″ Diamond

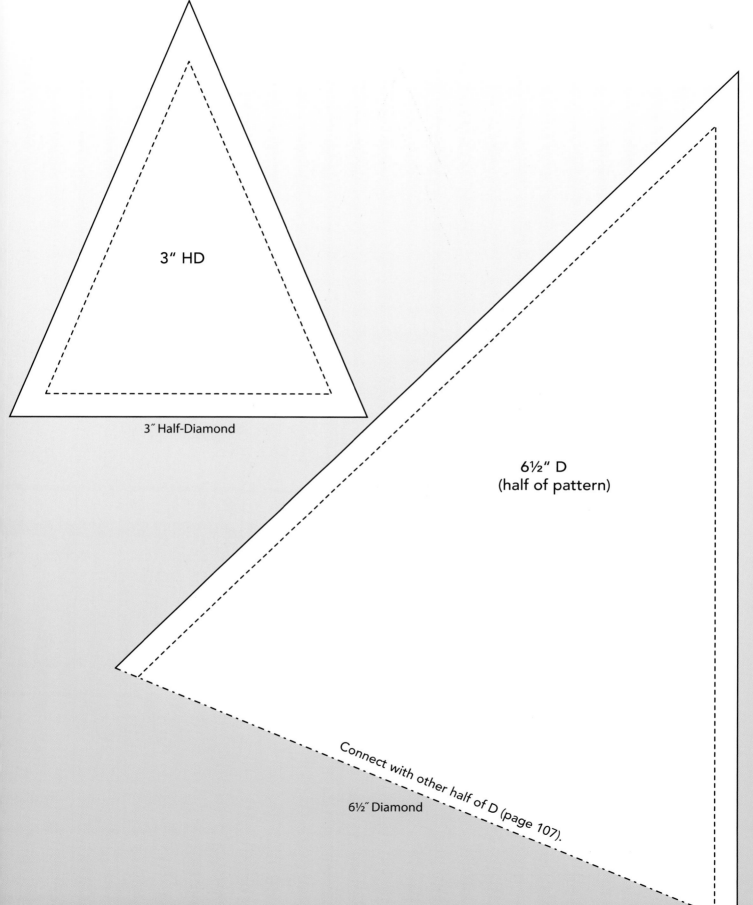

3" HD

3″ Half-Diamond

6½" D
(half of pattern)

Connect with other half of D (page 107).

6½″ Diamond

6½″ HD

6½″ Half-Diamond

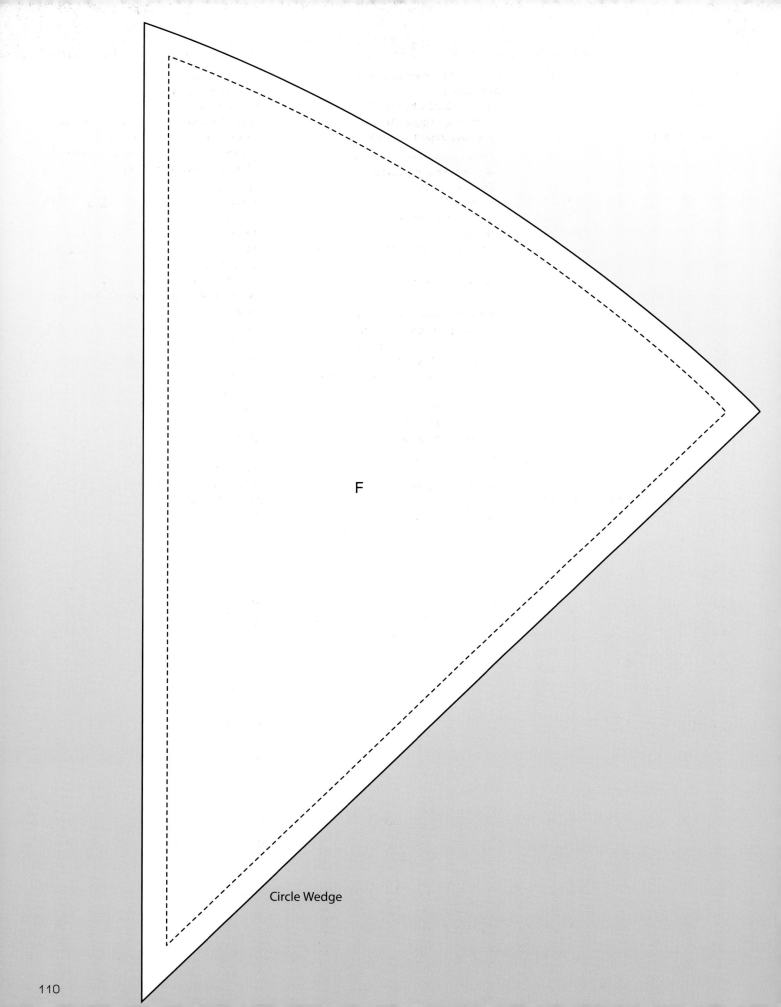

F

Circle Wedge

RESOURCES

For a list of other fine books from C&T Publishing, ask for a free catalog:

C&T Publishing, Inc.
P.O. Box 1456
Lafayette, CA 94549
(800) 284-1114
Email: ctinfo@ctpub.com
Website: www.ctpub.com
C&T Publishing's professional photography services are now available to the public. Visit us at www.ctmediaservices.com.

For quilting supplies:
Cotton Patch
1025 Brown Ave.
Lafayette, CA 94549
Store: (925) 284-1177
Mail order: (925) 283-7883
Email: CottonPa@aol.com
Website: www.quiltusa.com
Note: fabrics used in the quilts shown may not be currently available, as fabric manufacturers keep most fabrics in print for only a short time.

Laundering/Dye Treatment Products
Dharma Trading Company
(www.dharmatrading.com)
  Dharma Dye Fixative
  Synthrapol
ProChemical & Dye (www.prochemical.com)
  Retayne

Grocery and department stores, laundry department
  Shout Color Catchers (USA)
  Woolite Dye Magnet (USA)
  Zero Dye Magnet (Canada)

Rotary Cutting Rulers, Mats, and Cutters
C&T Publishing (www.ctpub.com)
  fast2cut® Fussy Cutter™ 45° diamond rulers: 3˝ and 6½˝
  fast2cut® Half- & Quarter-Diamond Ruler Set
Omnigrid
  Invisi-Grip transparent film prevents ruler slippage
Creative Grids USA
Olfa

Sewing Machine Manufacturers
  Bernina (www.berninausa.com)
  Brother (www.brother-usa.com)
  Elna (www.elna.com)
  Husqvarna/Viking (www.husqvarnaviking.com)
  Janome (www.janome.com)
  Pfaff (www.pfaff.com)
  Singer (www.singer.com)

Fabric Manufacturers
  Alexander Henry (www.ahfabrics.com)
  Hoffman of California (www.hoffmanfabrics.com)
  P & B Textiles (www.pbtex.com)
  Robert Kaufman (www.robertkaufman.com)

Timeless Treasures Fabrics (www.ttfabrics.com)
Thread Manufacturers
  A&E – Signature Thread (www.amefird.com)
  Sulky of America (www.sulky.com)
  Superior Thread (www.superiorthread.com)
  YLI Corp. (www.ylicorp.com)

Sewing Notions Sources
  Clover Quilting and Sewing Notions (www.clover-usa.com)
  Needles, pins, seam rippers, awls, marking tools, snippers and scissors, rotary cutters, thimbles, rulers
  June Tailor (www.junetailor.com)
  Nancy's Notions (www.nancysnotions.com)
  Perkins Dry Goods (www.perkinsdrygoods.com)
  Perfect Piecing Seam Guide
  Prym-Dritz (www.dritz.com)

Fusible Adhesives and Stabilizers
The Warm Company
  Steam-a-Seam Lite
  Steam-a-Seam II Lite
Pellon
  Wonder Under (USA)
  Bondaweb (UK)
Esterita Austin's Misty Fuse
Therm O Web, Inc.
  Heat 'n Bond Lite

About the Author

JAN KRENTZ is a nationally recognized quilt instructor, author, and designer. Winner of the 1998 Teacher of the Year award from *Professional Quilter Magazine,* Jan's motivating presentations and workshops are packed with practical tips, techniques, and methods to ensure success. Jan is the author of *Lone Star Quilts & Beyond, Hunter Star Quilts & Beyond,* and *Diamond Quilts and Beyond,* and designer of the fast2cut® Fussy Cutter™ diamond tools (all available from C&T Publishing). Jan lives with her husband, Don, in Poway, California.

Visit Jan's website, www.jankrentz.com; contact her by email, jan@jankrentz.com; or write to Jan by postal mail:

Jan Krentz
P.O. Box 686
Poway, CA 92074-0686

Great Titles
from C&T PUBLISHING

Paula Nadelstern's
KALEIDOSCOPE QUILTS
An Artist's Journey Continues

One-Block Wonders encore!
New Shapes, Multiple Fabrics, Out-of-this-World Quilts
MAXINE ROSENTHAL & JOY PELZMANN

STUNNING ANGLEPLAY QUILTS
• 6 PROJECTS • 42 EXCITING BLOCKS • EASY, NO-MATH PIECING
MARGARET J. MILLER

Radiant Sunshine & Shadow
23 QUILTS WITH NINE-PATCH SPARKLE
Helen Frost & Catherine Skow

3-in-1 NEW & IMPROVED COLOR TOOL
NEW & IMPROVED 3-in-1 COLOR TOOL
NOW INCLUDES THESE MUST-HAVE TOOLS!
• Numbered Swatches
• Two Value Finders Green and Red
PLUS
• Color Guide
• Fabric Preview Windows
IDEAL FOR:
Quilting
Crafts
Home décor
Knitting
Sewing
Scrapbooking
Floral design
Graphic design!
JOEN WOLFROM

Carol Doak's Simply Sensational 9-Patch Stars
BONUS Foundation Factory CD Included
• 12 QUILT PROJECTS • MIX & MATCH UNITS TO CREATE A GALAXY OF PAPER-PIECED STARS